The Promise-Powered Life *for Women*

How to See the Promises of God Fulfilled in Your Life

J. M. FARRO

Copyright © 2014 by J. M. FARRO
P.O. Box 434
Nazareth, PA 18064

ISBN-10: 1497571502

ISBN-13: 978-1497571501

Acknowledgements

I would like to take this opportunity to thank my husband, Joe, for helping me to put this project together, and for faithfully reading and editing my devotionals on a regular basis. I could not devote myself to my ministry work without his constant support and understanding. He has been my best friend and confidant for more than 40 years.

Many thanks to my sister, Jeannine, for the many hours she dedicated to proofreading this book, and providing her input.

I also sincerely appreciate my son, Joseph, and all of the valuable technical support and computer help he has given me over the years. His expertise, confidence, and calmness in stressful times have been a great inspiration and encouragement to me.

A special thanks to my son, John, who has allowed me to serve on the staff of his extraordinary ministry, Jesusfreakhideout.com, for the past 16 years. I am ever so grateful to him for telling me those many years ago, "Mom, you should write some devotionals for my site..."

Cover Photo by Joseph DiBiase II

Introduction

When I got serious about my relationship with Christ more than twenty years ago, and began an in-depth study of the Scriptures, I discovered that I had inherited a wealth of promises from God Himself. I also discovered that these divine promises are not automatic. They have to be claimed and received by faith.

As I sought the Lord about receiving the full benefit of His promises, He showed me His instructions in Isaiah 62:6-7 (AMP): "You who [are His servants and by your prayers] put the Lord in remembrance [of His promises], keep not silence, and give Him no rest..." One of the best ways to activate the power and benefits of God's supernatural promises is to pray them back to the Lord. When we do this, we are in effect telling Him, "Lord, this is what You said, and I'm trusting You to keep Your Word."

Since I began making my prayers promise-centered, instead of problem-centered, I have seen my percentage of answered prayer increase dramatically. Why? Because when we pray God's promises, we are praying God's will. And the Bible says that "if we ask anything according to His will, He hears us," and we can be confident "that we have what we asked of Him". (1 John 5:14-15 NIV)

The Lord has given His children promises of provision, protection, power, deliverance, life, healing, strength, wisdom, peace, joy, victory, success, wholeness, freedom, and everything we need to live the abundant life in Christ, and to fulfill our God-given purpose and potential on this earth.

Scripture says that Jesus "carries out and fulfills all of God's promises, no matter how many of them there are". (2 Corinthians 1:20 TLB) I encourage you to dig into God's Word, asking the Lord to lead you to the promises that pertain to your specific needs. Believe them. Pray them. Claim them as your own. Then watch God go to work to prove His faithfulness every time!

Table of Contents

HE MAKES ALL THINGS NEW 1

DIFFICULT DELAYS 5

CHANGED HEARTS 9

ESCAPE TEMPTATION'S POWER...13

JOY AND STRENGTH FOR OUR WORK 17

FROM MISERY TO MINISTRY 21

OUR GOOD GIFT GIVER..25

FRUITFUL OR FRAZZLED? 29

WHAT IT MEANS TO TRUST GOD 33

A FEW WORDS ABOUT WEIGHT MANAGEMENT 37

EQUIPPED FOR SERVICE 41

DIVINE DEALS 45

OUR "NEW THING" GOD..49

GET SPECIFIC WITH YOUR PRAYERS 53

THE POWER AND RESPONSIBILITY OF AGREEMENT 57

I STILL HAVE A LOT TO BE THANKFUL FOR............................61

GOD'S CARE IN TIMES OF CRISIS 65

THE POWER OF POSITIVE SPEECH 69

RESPONDING TO REBELS 73

GOD'S GREATER POWER...77

BETTER TO TRUST THE LORD...81

THE RECIPE FOR ABUNDANT JOY 85

CONSIDER HIM FAITHFUL 89

HOW ANGER HARMS...93

BLESSINGS WE DON'T DESERVE 101

PEACE OF MIND AND HEART...105

REALIZE YOUR HOPES AND DREAMS.................................109

DECISIONS AND DILEMMAS...113

GET OUT OF THE WAY..117

THE PAIN OF LOSS 121

DATING: ONE MOM'S PERSPECTIVE 125

DON'T FAIL TO ASK 129

YOU DON'T HAVE TO BE AFRAID.....................................133

EXCUSES OR FREEDOM? 137

THE REWARDS OF ENDURANCE 141

A GOD OF DELIVERANCES 145

FASTING FOR FREEDOM..149

SUBMIT TO GOD'S GOOD PLANS.....................................153

THE BEST PLACE FOR BURDENS.......................................157

OPPORTUNITIES AND ADVERSARIES 161

HOLDING ON TO OUR HEALING 165

FREE FROM CONDEMNATION 169

A LIFETIME SAVIOR..173

BENEFITS AND BLESSINGS FROM GOD 177

OUR SAVIOR IN THE STORM 181

THE FEAR OF MAN 185

THE GOD WHO HEARS AND ANSWERS.............................189

YOU DON'T NEED ANY HELPERS......................................193

GOOD NEWS VS. BAD NEWS..195

ABOUT THE AUTHOR 199

He Makes All Things New

"Then He who sat on the throne said, 'Behold, I make all things new.'" Revelation 21:5 NKJV

When I heard that some friends of mine went through a harrowing and messy divorce, it grieved my heart. My husband and I had known this couple for close to 40 years, almost the whole time that Joe and I had been together. I couldn't shake the feelings of shock and discouragement after hearing the news, so I sought the Lord in prayer about it. "I don't get it, Lord. These friends of mine always seemed like the perfect couple. What happened?" As I listened intently for the Lord's answer, I sensed Him saying to my heart, "They forgot why they fell in love in the first place."

I knew very well what the Lord meant by those words. I had seen many couples over the years lose their appreciation for each other. And I had been guilty of the same mistake myself. It wasn't until my husband had a heart attack, and then open-heart surgery, that I realized just how much I had been taking him for granted. I asked God to forgive me for failing to cherish the wonderful man He had given me, and I asked Him what I could do to make it up to my husband. The Lord impressed upon my heart that He was prepared to renew my marriage, and to make it better than ever before, but that I was going to have to do my part. That's when He led me to begin meditating on how Joe and I met, and why we fell in love.

I started thinking about how Joe and I were in the same sociology class in college, and how our professor chose us to be in a skit together. Our assignment called for us to spend time with each other apart from the rest of the class, so we began talking, and Joe mentioned that he had a new car. When he asked if I'd like to see it, I said yes, and we ended up going out to lunch together. That led to us going to dinner that evening, and though I was usually a rather private person, I ended up telling Joe my entire life story. Before the evening ended, Joe announced, "I think I'll marry you!" I laughed when he said it, but his words warmed my heart, and drew me close to him.

The Lord was right. The more I thought about our "love story," the more my love and appreciation for my husband deepened, even though more than 40 years have passed since the day we met. And as I demonstrated newfound respect and admiration for Joe, it became clear that his love was deepening for me. In the Book of Revelation, Jesus says, "Behold, I make all things new." (Revelation 21:5 NKJV) I've discovered that the Lord is more than willing and able to make relationships and marriages new when we ask Him to, and when we agree to do our part in the process. I can't help thinking about all of the marriages that could have been saved if the husband and wife had only sought God's help, and had agreed to work with Him and each other.

Whether you have been married for a year or 40 years, or even more, I urge you to keep your own "love story" alive by keeping it in your thoughts, and allowing it to draw you closer to your spouse. Most of all, keep your marriage covered in prayer, and partner with the Lord for its protection. Then watch God do His part to bless it, and to make it new each and every day!

Lord, thank You for my spouse. Forgive me when I have taken him for granted, and when I've failed to treat him with the respect that he deserves. I ask that You renew our relationship and our marriage, and make them better and stronger than before. Show us what our part is in the process, and help us to do it faithfully. Today, I commit to keeping our "love story" in my heart and mind every day!

Promise-Power Point: God is willing and able to make my marriage new again, as I demonstrate my willingness to do my part with His help.

Difficult Delays

"But these things I plan won't happen right away. Slowly, steadily, surely, the time approaches when the vision will be fulfilled. If it seems slow, do not despair, for these things will surely come to pass. Just be patient! They will not be overdue a single day!"
Habakkuk 2:3 TLB

About two years into my devotional writing ministry, I was getting so much positive feedback from my readers that one of my friends convinced me to begin contacting publishers, to see if they would be interested in putting my messages into book form. So I set about writing letters to publishers, and sending them a collection of my devotionals. After weeks of hard work and high hopes, all I got in return were rejection notices. For a long time afterwards, I was plagued with feelings of discouragement and disappointment. I constantly prayed that the Lord would give me the strength and endurance to stay at my post, and to complete the assignment He gave me, no matter how long it took. But time and time again, I asked myself, "Why am I doing this? Does anyone really care? Why should I keep going?"

Thankfully, I discovered the promising verse above in the book of Habakkuk. Here, the Lord was reassuring me that even though my hopes and dreams would not be fulfilled right away, they would surely come to pass if I would be patient and refuse to despair – and if I would not abandon my post. And they would be right on time – not according to my timetable, but according to God's. He alone knows the best time to answer our prayers, and when the answer will profit us most.

Exactly two years later, I contacted one of the same publishers a second time, and this time, they were enthusiastic about my devotionals. In fact, they were so excited about my work that they gave me three books at one time, instead of just one. My dream to become a published author had finally been fulfilled, and God brought it to fruition in such a way that it exceeded my highest expectations.

Perhaps you have experienced some difficult delays of your own. Remember this, dear one – where God is concerned, delays are not necessarily denials. Many times, when your prayers go unanswered, He is not telling you "no". On the contrary, many times He is saying to you, "Wait. I have something even better in store for you. Trust Me. Work with Me. And you will see it come to pass!"

Lord, I confess that sometimes I become impatient and discouraged when things don't happen as quickly as I would like them to. Help me to seek You continually for strength, endurance, and everything I need to wait on You with peace and joy in my heart. Remove from me every hope and dream that is not of You, so that I don't spend my life waiting for things that will never come to pass. Thank You that as I live for You, and follow Your lead, my dreams and visions won't be overdue a single day!

Promise-Power Point: If I will refuse to allow difficult delays to sidetrack me when I am doing the work God has called me to do, He will exceed my highest expectations in fulfilling my hopes and dreams.

Changed Hearts

"The king's heart is in the hand of the Lord, like the rivers of water; He turns it wherever He wishes."
Proverbs 21:1 NKJV

It's been rightly said that our God is a God of hearts. That means that, not only does the Lord see inside our hearts, but He can also change hearts as well. The verse above assures us that God can, and will, direct people's hearts so that His plans and purposes prevail — especially when His children are praying and trusting Him to intervene in a matter. I have seen the Lord cause a change of heart in the most stubborn and rebellious of people. And I have seen Him do it so many times that I am no longer discouraged when it seems as though someone will never change.

Very often, God will use someone or something as an instrument of change in a person's decisions, desires, or course of action. My husband, Joe, and I experienced this very thing two summers ago, when our 8-year-old pet duck, Lily, died. At first, Joe and I were so grieved that we decided that we wouldn't even try to get a new mate for our duck, Larry. But when Larry started becoming lethargic, and refused to eat, we knew that we needed to begin searching for a new female. When we earnestly prayed that God would lead us to the perfect new pet, the Lord reminded us that we had given ducklings to a certain local farm in the past.

However, when we approached the farmer, Jake, and asked if he would give us one of his ducks so we could take it home to Larry, he refused.

We continued to pray for God's guidance in the matter, and we explored every avenue that we could think of, but our efforts to find a new mate for Larry repeatedly failed. Once again, we approached Jake the farmer and asked if he would consider parting with one of his ducks, and once again he refused. Joe and I were beginning to think that perhaps it wasn't the Lord's will for us to get another pet. Then suddenly, we discovered a bird farm about an hour away from us that had some ducks for sale. When we got there, the only female duck we saw that was about Larry's size was a beautiful black Muscovy. We decided to take her home with us, but when we introduced her to Larry, he wanted nothing to do with her. Now we had two unhappy ducks, instead of just one.

We discovered from fellow duck owners that because Larry was so old — twelve years, to be exact — he was not likely to accept a mate of a different breed. My husband and I both agreed that we couldn't keep our new female. And since Joe refused to drive an hour to return her to the bird farm we got her from, we decided to offer her to farmer Jake. When we arrived at the farm, and handed our female over to Jake, he was so impressed with her beautiful black feathers and gentle demeanor that he insisted that we take one of his females for a mate for Larry. Joe and I were stunned, and we gratefully brought home a pretty little brown duck that we named Libby. For Libby and Larry, it was love at first sight, and they have spent every moment together ever since.

If you long to see someone have a change of heart, I urge you to pray about it and commit the matter to God. Just as the Lord used a little black duck to turn a man's heart in my situation, He will do whatever is necessary to effect a change in your circumstances, so that His purpose will prevail, and He will be glorified!

Lord, I thank You for being a God of hearts, and for being willing and able to change people's hearts when we pray and trust You to intervene. Reveal to me what hearts and situations You desire to effect a change in right now. Help me to see these people and things through Your eyes, so that a lack of faith won't stand in the way of the work You long to do. Today, I choose to believe Your promise, and to look to You to turn and direct hearts for my good and Your glory!

Promise-Power Point: *I will witness changed hearts and circumstances when I claim God's promise in faith, seek the Lord's direction, and follow His lead.*

Escape Temptation's Power

"Remember this — the wrong desires that come into your life aren't anything new and different. Many others have faced exactly the same problems before you. And no temptation is irresistible. You can trust God to keep the temptation from becoming so strong that you can't stand up against it, for He has promised this and will do what He says. He will show you how to escape temptation's power so that you can bear up patiently against it." 1 Corinthians 10:13 TLB

I hear from a lot of dear Christian people who struggle with ungodly habits, and my heart goes out to them. I love praying for these folks, and standing in faith with them for their deliverance. I long to see them experiencing the blessed freedom that belongs to them in Christ. While I don't profess to have "arrived," I have made amazing progress in almost every area of my life, as I have taken God at His Word, and cooperated with Him for my spiritual growth.

One thing that has helped me to determine what areas I most need to work with God in, is to think about Romans 7:20 (NIV): "Now if I do what I do not want to do, it is no longer I who do it, but it is sin living in me that does it." In other words, when you and I do something we really don't want to do — even something we HATE doing — it's sin living in us that compels us to do it. The good news is that once we have surrendered our hearts to Christ, and committed ourselves to live His way, we no longer have to bow down to sin, or to the temptations that the devil and his dark forces send our way. Here is the truth of the matter: "We know that our old sinful selves were crucified with Christ so that sin might lose its power in our lives. We are no longer slaves to sin. For when we died with Christ we were set free from the power of sin." (Romans 6:6-7 NLT) Did you get that? You and I no longer have to cave in to pressure from the world, our flesh, or the devil to do what we know we shouldn't do.

For example, there are times when I am not really hungry, but my flesh will crave something to eat because I have seen or smelled something good. When I am following the Spirit of God's promptings – and I am being totally honest with myself – I will say to myself, "I don't even want that!" My real self, my spirit – the part of me that is united with Christ – won't want to feed my body more than it wants or needs, because I know that the consequences of continually giving in to my flesh will be negative and harmful to me.

Staying on the subject of eating for a moment, let me share with you what God has shown me in this area. First of all, let's acknowledge that food is always all around us. And since we have to eat to survive and thrive, we are always going to be exposed to the temptation to overeat, and to eat the wrong things. An important key to this problem is found in First Corinthians 10:13 (TLB): "Remember this – the wrong desires that come into your life aren't anything new and different. Many others have faced exactly the same problems before you. And no temptation is irresistible. You can trust God to keep the temptation from becoming so strong that you can't stand up against it, for He has promised this and will do what He says. He will show you how to escape temptation's power so that you can bear up patiently against it." Don't miss the part that says, "NO temptation is irresistible." Just that one little truth has the power to set you free from anything and everything that holds you captive today, if choose to believe it and act on it. Where does every temptation originate? In our minds. And that's where we can interrupt the process of temptation that leads to sin. I happen to love hot chocolate. But drinking too much of it is bad for my health and my waistline. So the Lord has shown me that the very second I begin to think about it, I must dismiss the thought of it. If I don't, I am in danger of acting on my thoughts, and following them to get myself a cup of it.

Scripture confirms that the battle takes place in our minds when it says: "For though we walk in the flesh, we do not war according to the flesh. For the weapons of our warfare are not carnal but mighty in God for pulling down strongholds, casting down arguments and every high thing that exalts itself against the knowledge of God, bringing every thought into captivity to the obedience of Christ." (2 Corinthians 10:3-5 NKJV) The moment we hesitate to "cast down" disobedient thoughts, we are in danger of carrying out the sinful actions that we so desperately want to resist.

Jesus promised, "If you abide in My word [hold fast to My teachings and live in accordance with them], you are truly My disciples. And you will know the Truth, and the Truth will set you free." (John 8:31-32 AMP) If you will lay hold of these truths today, and if you will apply them to your life with the help of the Holy Spirit who dwells in you, you will experience the blessed freedom that can only come from Christ!

Lord, thank You that it's Your heartfelt desire for me to walk in total freedom every day of my life. Teach me how to fully cooperate with You to that end. Show me how to interrupt the process of temptation that leads me into sin. Remind me that because of Your grace, no temptation can be irresistible to me. Help me to immediately cast down every wrong thought, instead of dwelling on it until it causes me to act wrongly. Today, I choose to resist the pull of the world, the flesh, and the devil that would keep me from fulfilling my God-given purpose and potential!

Promise-Power Point: When I believe and act on the truth that I am no longer a slave to sin, but that I was set free from the power of sin, I will experience the supernatural freedom that Christ purchased for me on the Cross.

Joy and Strength for Our Work

"She sets about her work vigorously; her arms are strong for her tasks." Proverbs 31:17 NIV

When the Lord showed me this verse of Scripture about 20 years ago, He began teaching me about the importance of being an energetic and enthusiastic worker. He made it clear to me that one reason why He gave me His indwelling Spirit when I received Christ as my Savior was so that I no longer had to dread or drag through my work. He showed me Ecclesiastes 5:19 (NLT), where Solomon says that enjoying our work is a gift from God. And it doesn't matter whether our work involves child care, office work, housework, yard work, ministry work, or anything else – we can enjoy it all, and we can do it energetically.

When I have a job to do that I am dreading, I ask for the Lord's help to get started, and then I declare, "I set about my work vigorously!" (Proverbs 31:17 NIV) This reminds me that I don't have to put off a job of mine simply because I'm not looking forward to it. God has equipped me to dig in to my projects, instead of procrastinating and causing them to intimidate me and gain control over me. When my job involves physical work, I declare the second half of this verse, saying, "My arms are strong for my tasks!" When we make these faith-filled declarations, we are alerting the Holy

Spirit to send waves of supernatural strength through our bodies, and to fill us with divine energy. The apostle Paul spoke of this powerful principle when he wrote that God filled him with "superhuman energy" for his work. (Colossians 1:29 AMP) Once I began experiencing this kind of energy years ago, I began claiming it on a regular basis, and relying on it for both big and small tasks. As I get older, I realize more and more the value of this kind of strength.

I love a clean house. Anyone who knows me knows how true this is. But there are certain aspects of housecleaning that I simply dread. One of them is mopping floors. So when I know that I have to do it, I ask the Lord for help, and without thinking about it, I get out my mop and pail. I begin filling the pail with water, and I pour in the detergent. And the next thing I know, I am mopping floors! You see, once we think too much about starting a task we don't particularly like, we give it power over us. God wants us to go ahead and take some steps toward beginning the task, without overthinking it. When we do, He gets involved and strengthens us until the job is completed. And if we ask and expect Him to, He will even fill us with joy while we do it.

Perhaps you dread going grocery shopping. I understand how you feel. But like I tell my husband, Joe, if you want food in the house, you've got to shop for it! What I like to do is to time myself when I shop. I use my smartphone to track my time, and I challenge myself to get in and out of the store quickly. This discourages me from spending too much time browsing, which can increase my shopping time by 30 minutes or more. Even though my husband is a browser – and I often have to tap him on the shoulder and tell him, "Focus!" – the last time we went to the supermarket, he said, "Let's time ourselves!" He's learned that getting in and out of the store quickly can make a task like this more enjoyable and productive, and less likely to become a source of dread.

The Bible says: "Commit everything you do to the Lord. Trust Him to help you do it and He will." (Psalm 37:5 TLB) I challenge you to begin inviting God into your tasks, no matter how simple or mundane they may be, and watch Him bless the work of your hands, and fill you with His joy!

Lord, I thank You for filling me with Your Holy Spirit, whom You called my "Helper". (John 14:16 NASB) Teach me how to rely on Your Spirit to strengthen and guide me through all of my work. Guard me from procrastination, and help me to set about my tasks "vigorously". Give me Your gift of joy for my work so that I can really enjoy it. (Ecclesiastes 5:19 NLT) Today, I choose to commit my work to You, to ask for Your help, and to trust You to equip me with everything I need to succeed!

Promise-Power Point: When I do my work God's way, in God's strength, I can perform my tasks with "superhuman energy" and with supernatural joy.

From Misery to Ministry

"Though You have made me see troubles, many and bitter, You will restore my life again; from the depths of the earth You will again bring me up. You will increase my honor and comfort me once again." Psalm 71:20-21 NIV

I hear regularly from women who are going through desperate times. Many of them have entered into unwise marriages that resulted in harrowing divorces which left them so destitute that they had to move in with their parents. When these women are mothers, it's particularly hard when their parents are a negative influence on their children. Often, these women have learned a lot from their suffering, and they are ready to give God first place in their lives. They know in their hearts that the Lord has good plans for them, but they still struggle with discouragement as their troubles threaten to drain them of their faith and joy.

If you see yourself in any aspect of this scenario, I have some words of encouragement for you today. Scripture says: "Though You have made me see troubles, many and bitter, You will restore my life again; from the depths of the earth You will again bring me up. You will increase my honor and comfort me once again." (Psalm 71:20-21 NIV) This is a personal promise from God that He is willing and able to turn your misery into your ministry, and your mess into your message. You see, God never wastes our pain, or the lessons we learn from our suffering. He not only causes us to profit from our difficult experiences, but He teaches us how to use them to build up others, and to lead them to Him. As God uses us to touch and change lives for His glory, He increases our honor, just like this promise says, and He gives us the comfort only divine love can offer.

I have lived a long time, and I have known the joys of being a happy wife, mother, and grandmother, but I have never experienced more joy than when the Most High God has used me to make an eternal difference in people's lives. If you have seen some dark days of your own, then you have the potential to have a tremendous impact on the lives of others for all eternity. But you must surrender your life to the Lord – along with all of your mistakes and misery – and ask Him to give you a new life and a fresh start. When you do, you will see Him fill your life with more purpose and meaning than you ever dreamed possible, and you will experience a joy that you have never known!

Lord, I confess that sometimes I get weary and worn out from the struggles of daily life. Please change my perspective so that I can see the value of my difficult experiences, and how You can use them to profit me and others. Lift me up and comfort me so that I won't be overcome by discouragement or despair. And give me the honor and blessings that can only come from You. From now on, I will look to You for my purpose, fulfillment, and peace!

Promise-Power Point: As I live my life for God, and commit all my trials and troubles to Him, He will turn my misery into my ministry, and I will make an eternal difference in people's lives for His glory.

Our Good Gift Giver

"Don't be deceived, my dear brothers and sisters. Every good and perfect gift is from above, coming down from the Father of the heavenly lights, who does not change like shifting shadows." James 1:16-17 NIV

I once suffered a bout of hearing loss that made it difficult for me to function, and that baffled even my doctors. I had been praying and standing on God's Word for my healing the whole time, but the trouble persisted. As I sought the Lord for His wisdom and strength one morning, He led me to call the prayer line of one of the ministries that I have supported over the years. A godly man who was well acquainted with the Scriptures answered the phone, and he prayed a prayer that changed my perspective, and enabled me to receive my healing. He said, "Lord, we thank You that this hearing loss is not from You. Therefore, we reject it, we rebuke it, and we command it to leave Joanne's body now and forever, in Jesus' name!"

If you had asked me if I thought that God might have somehow been responsible for my affliction, I would have emphatically said "no". But apparently, the Lord knew that I needed some reassurance in this area, so He sent this godly man to provide it. When he declared that my hearing loss was not from God, I felt a certain relief and release in my spirit. And I began taking this man's words of faith as my own, and commanding my affliction to leave, on the basis and belief that the Lord wanted me healed and whole.

You see, Satan is a deceiver. In fact, Jesus called him "the father of lies". When we are sick or hurting in some way, the devil will try to convince us that God is responsible for our misery because He is a sadist, and He loves to see us suffer. But God's Word says otherwise. In fact, Acts 10:38 (NASB) says: "You know of Jesus of Nazareth, how God anointed Him with the Holy Spirit and with power, and how He went about doing good and healing all who were oppressed by the devil, for God was with Him." There are many Scriptures that tell us the truth about God and His Son, and their good intentions for us. It may sound simple, but the truth is that God is good, and the devil is bad. Jesus said that Satan "comes only to steal and kill and destroy." (John 10:10 NIV) On the other hand, the Bible tells us plainly, "The Son of God came to destroy the works of the devil." (1 John 3:8 NLT)

James wrote: "Don't be deceived, my dear brothers and sisters. Every good and perfect gift is from above, coming down from the Father of the heavenly lights, who does not change like shifting shadows." (James 1:16-17 NIV) James didn't want us to be deceived about God's intentions for us. He wanted us to know that God is a good God, and that He always has our best interests at heart. But we must remember that we live in a fallen, broken world. And there will be times when we unwittingly open the door for Satan and his evil cohorts to do us harm, through our own disobedience. But even during those times, our God is eager to help us and heal us when we turn to Him in heartfelt repentance.

My misconception of God hindered and delayed my healing. Don't you make the same mistake.

Lord, when I am sick or suffering in some way, help me to see You as the good and gracious God You really are. Show me how to receive the healing and deliverance You have for me. Remind me that my lack of trust in You can cause me to delay or forfeit my rescue. Teach me how to resist the devil's temptations and tactics, and lead me to defeat him every time. Thank You for sending Jesus so that I could live the abundant life! (John 10:10)

Promise-Power Point: God is a good God, and He sends me good gifts. When I see Him and His intentions from the proper perspective, I will open the door to receive His best in every area of my life, and in every situation.

Fruitful or Frazzled?

"For it is not [intended] that other people be eased and relieved [of their responsibility] and you be burdened and suffer [unfairly]." 2 Corinthians 8:13 AMP

There is a serious problem among Christians these days that grieves my heart, and I believe it also grieves the heart of God. Too many of God's people are taking on responsibilities that are too much for them — responsibilities that the Lord never expected or wanted them to accept. Sometimes, these well-meaning, but misguided, people commit themselves to performing tasks, activities, or errands that are completely out of the will of God for them. Other times, they neglect to put boundaries and limits on the work that the Lord has, in fact, assigned them. And the result can be disastrous. Often, their health suffers. Or their relationships become strained. They may even harbor bitterness and resentment toward the people they feel are taking advantage of them. In some cases, they may even become angry at God. If you recognize yourself in any of these descriptions, don't feel condemned. All of us have fallen into this trap of the enemy at one time or another. I certainly have. But there's a better way. Let's look at what the Word of God has to say on this subject.

The apostle Paul wrote: "Our desire is not that others might be relieved while you are hard pressed, but that there might be equality." (2 Corinthians 8:13 NIV) Paul was referring to financial giving here, but the Lord has shown me that this principle can apply to the giving of our time and energy, too. What this means is that while we are called to serve others – especially others in need – we should never serve them to the point where they are "relieved," but we are "hard pressed". Human nature being what it is, people can be extremely selfish. They may focus on their own needs, and expect and accept help from others, without regard for the other person's well-being. Then, the servant becomes hard pressed and worn out, and they risk becoming useless to everyone, including themselves and God.

Solomon wrote about the righteous woman: "She considers a [new] field before she buys or accepts it [expanding prudently and not courting neglect of her present duties by assuming other duties]." (Proverbs 31:16 AMP) Did you get that? This wise woman "considers" before she makes commitments. She is careful not to "assume other duties" that will cause her to "neglect her present duties". She thinks things through. And she undoubtedly consults God. Too often, you and I take on new responsibilities and assignments that the Lord never intended us to. We see someone in need and we think, "That person could use some help. I'm a Christian, and I'm sure God would want me to help them." It sounds righteous and noble, but if we haven't consulted the Lord in the matter, and we just used our own logic or reasoning, we could very well step out of the will of God. And we will regret our decision in the end. The second part of this verse says: "With her savings [of time and strength] she plants fruitful vines in her vineyard." The bottom line is that we are called to be fruitful for the Lord. But we can sacrifice our productiveness for God when we fail to use our "time and strength" wisely.

So how do we make sure that we are not out of the will of God with our commitments? We seek the Lord for His wisdom and guidance. "If you need wisdom – if you want to know what God wants you to do – ask Him, and He will gladly tell you. He will not resent your asking. But when you ask Him, be sure that you really expect Him to answer..." (James 1:5-6 NLT) The Lord cares very much how you use your time and energy, and He will tell you how to spend them wisely when you claim His promises, and expect to hear from Him. One of the best ways to become sensitive and obedient to God's voice is to spend regular time alone with Him – praying and reading His Word, and listening intently for His answers. Constant noise and busyness can make it nearly impossible to hear from God clearly. But when we practice regular periods of stillness and attentiveness, we will be amazed at how the Lord reveals Himself and His will for us. I am writing this message today because I care about you, and I don't want you to spend the rest of your life weary and worn out. I want you to be fruitful for the Lord, so that you can experience the truly abundant, fulfilling, and satisfying life that He's called you to!

Lord, forgive me for the times that I have overextended myself and taken on responsibilities that were not Your best for me. I repent for the times I used my time and energy unwisely, and sacrificed my fruitfulness for You. Teach me how to consult You before I commit to new responsibilities or assignments. And show me how to establish proper boundaries and limits, so that my health and well-being won't suffer. Thank You that as I seek You and follow Your lead in this area, I will live the life of peace and purpose that belongs to me in Christ!

Promise-Power Point: God Himself will show me how to avoid living a "hard pressed" life, when I seek Him and consult Him about how to spend my time and energy on a regular basis.

What it means to Trust God

"All those who know Your mercy, Lord, will count on You for help. For You have never yet forsaken those who trust in You." Psalm 9:10 TLB

When I first discovered that I needed to have surgery for an affliction that was supposed to have been taken care of by a previous surgery, I confess that I was initially stunned and in denial. Fortunately, I have made a habit of seeking God first when trouble strikes, so I got alone with Him and asked Him to speak words of consolation to my heart. The first thing He showed me was that I was NOT to wallow in self-pity, or to dwell on negative thoughts. Then He led me to seek out promises from His Word that would fill me with a fresh sense of hope for my situation. It was then that He reminded me of His words in Jeremiah 29:11 (NIV) which say: "'For I know the plans I have for you,' declares the LORD, 'plans to prosper you and not to harm you, plans to give you hope and a future.'" Though I had heard and read this verse many times over the years, the Holy Spirit gave it a fresh anointing for me, that filled me with a supernatural hope, peace, and joy that I really needed at the time. And I began to declare many times a day, "God is good, and His plans for me are good!" I knew that the Lord was teaching me anew about how important it was for me to put my wholehearted trust in Him. You see, the best way for us to forfeit God's best for us in any situation is to fail to trust Him the way He desires and deserves. That's why the enemy of our souls, Satan, works so hard to get us to doubt the Lord's love and good intentions for us.

What does it mean to trust God? First, we must believe that He is in control. The Bible says: "The Lord has established His throne in the heavens, and His sovereignty rules over all." (Psalm 103:19 NASB) If you don't firmly believe that God is the Creator and Ruler of the universe, then when you are in a trial of some sort, you will not believe that He is truly able to deliver you, no matter how bleak your circumstances look. If God is truly sovereign, does that mean that everything that happens in this world is His perfect will? Absolutely not. If that were the case, Jesus would never have instructed us to pray, "Your will be done, on earth as it is in heaven". (Matthew 6:10 NASB) Remember that God has given man a free will, so often He will permit what man permits. Also, just as the Lord has good plans for people, the dark forces in this earth have evil plans. (John 10:10) But there is hope. When a follower of Christ earnestly prays for protection and provision for himself or someone else, it can move the hand of God in mighty ways for the good of all. (James 5:16)

Trusting God also means that we believe He always has our best interests in mind. The Bible says: "The goodness of God endures continually." (Psalm 52:1 NKJV) If you ever doubt God's goodness, look at the Cross of Christ. Who else would sacrifice his only child to die a gruesome death for people who scorned him and his good intentions? But Jesus didn't die simply so that you and I could spend eternity with Him in heaven. He died so that we could "have and ENJOY life" right here and now. (John 10:10 AMP) And He is prepared to give us everything we need to live the life He has called us to, when we love Him, seek Him, and serve Him with all our hearts. As the apostle Paul wrote: "He who did not withhold or spare [even] His own Son but gave Him up for us all, will He not also with Him freely and graciously give us all [other] things?" (Romans 8:32 AMP)

And trusting God also means that we believe He will arrange things for our good, and His glory. Not everything that happens to us will be good. But God is good. And when we surrender our hearts and lives to Him, and follow His ways, we can expect Him to orchestrate events and circumstances so that they will profit us somehow. His solemn promise to His faithful ones says "that God causes all things to work together for good to those who love God, to those who are called according to His purpose." (Romans 8:28 NASB) The Lord will even change the hearts of people around us to work His perfect will in our lives, and to enable us to receive all the good things He has in store for us.

In a time of great trouble and anguish, David the shepherd-king declared, "I trusted in the LORD when I said, 'I am greatly afflicted.'" (Psalm 116:10 NIV) When I made this declaration of faith my own in my time of trial, it lifted me up and drew me close to God and His delivering power. Are you ready to put your trust in the Lord, and receive every good thing He has for you?

Lord, I no longer want to live with doubt and fear in my life, so I ask You to help me to cooperate with You for the building of my faith. When trouble strikes, remind me to turn to You first. Help me to believe that no matter what comes my way, You always have a custom-made solution for my problems. When circumstances seem frightening to me, reveal Yourself to me in healing, comforting, and life-changing ways. Today, I choose to believe in Your incomparable power, goodness, and love!

Promise-Power Point: I will never fail to reap God's very best outcome in any situation as long as I am trusting in Him, and following His lead.

A Few Words About Weight Management

"If any of you lacks wisdom, you should ask God, who gives generously to all without finding fault, and it will be given to you." James 1:5 NIV

During the Christmas season last year, I confess that I overdid it with my eating, and by the time the New Year rang in, my clothes were tighter than they have been in years. I decided to spend some extra time alone with the Lord, seeking His wisdom, and asking Him for some new strategies that would help me to gain some control over my eating. The first thing He imparted to me was that I was not giving enough attention to the spiritual aspect of this battle. I was so focused on the practical means of weight management, that I failed to remind myself often enough that Satan does not want me healthy and fit. Now, I have never encouraged people to be "devil-minded," but I must tell you that once I began to view the temptations that came my way as Satan's attempt to ruin my health, it totally changed my perspective, and I was able to say "no" more often when I was faced with opportunities to overeat, or to eat unwisely. Next, God gave me three strategies to consider when I was tempted to eat when I wasn't really hungry.

The first is: *Get a drink!* Sometimes, we can think we are hungry, when the truth is that we are only thirsty, and our bodies need to be hydrated. Filtered water may be your best option at these times, but pray about other healthy options that could satisfy your thirst. In my case, I find that having a cup of tea not only quenches my thirst, but it often curbs my appetite, too. God will show you which drinks are best for you, if you ask Him.

The second is: *Get some rest!* Many times, our body will signal that it needs more food when all it really needs is some rest and relaxation. This has been the greatest challenge for me personally. And the Lord is teaching me to force myself to take a break from what I'm doing, even if it's just for a few minutes, so that I won't give in to false hunger cravings because of feeling fatigued. God has also dealt with me about staying up too late. We can be very vulnerable at the end of the night when we are not only extremely tired, but a part of us wants to delay going to sleep. I have found that it helps to remind myself that I sleep so much better when I don't eat too close to bedtime.

Third is: *Get busy!* Sometimes, when we feel false hunger urges, we are actually bored, and we need to get busy doing something productive. A sense of accomplishment can be very uplifting and healing, while feeling like we've been wasting time can be deflating and discouraging. Those negative feelings can set us up for a bout of overeating. Also, it can be very easy to use food to delay performing a task that we aren't looking forward to. Food can be used as a very effective tool for procrastination. We need to remind ourselves that we are better off digging into our task right away, rather than asking ourselves if we feel like doing it, and putting it off. Praying for God's help to get started with our work can eliminate this problem amazingly fast.

One more thing. Don't be so afraid of wasting food that you wind up eating more than you should. I assure you that the Lord would rather have you throw food away than consume amounts that cause you to put on unhealthy pounds. God cares more about you than He cares about food. Your body is not a garbage can, but the temple of the Holy Spirit of God. (1 Corinthians 6:19-20) The Lord promises in His Word that He will give you wisdom when you ask Him for it in faith. (James 1:5) Today, I encourage you to seek Him about your eating habits, and ask Him for some divine strategies of your own!

Lord, remind me often that Satan "comes only to steal, kill, and destroy," and that it is his plan to keep me from living a long, healthy life. (John 10:10) I believe that You, on the other hand, have only good plans for my life, so I ask You to give me some effective strategies that will help me to control my eating and my weight. Teach me how to know the difference between real hunger and false hunger, and how to respond appropriately to each one. Take away my desire and my tendency to overeat, and to eat unwisely. On the basis of Your Word, I ask that You "feed me with the food You prescribe for me". (Proverbs 30:8 NKJV) I pray that whether I eat or drink, or whatever I do, I'll do it all for the glory of God! (1 Corinthians 10:31)

Promise-Power Point: God has specific and unique strategies to enable me to live a long, healthy life through proper weight management, and He will reveal them to me as I seek Him with an obedient and willing heart.

Equipped for Service

"Each of you should use whatever gift you have received to serve others, as faithful stewards of God's grace in its various forms. If anyone speaks, they should do so as one who speaks the very words of God. If anyone serves, they should do so with the strength God provides, so that in all things God may be praised through Jesus Christ." 1 Peter 4:10-11 NIV

When my son, Joseph, started a Bible Club at his high school, I offered to help out by driving home every student who needed a ride after the weekly meetings. I didn't want a single student to miss out on attending, simply because they lacked transportation. Because I was a stay-at-home mom, and my son was leading the club, I felt it was my duty to lend my assistance somehow. Every week, I made several trips between the school and the students' homes, filling up my car each time. Often, I was on the road for hours. It was hard work, but it gave me the opportunity to get to know many of these kids, and to listen to them, and minister to them.

After my son, Joseph, graduated from high school, my son, John, took over the leadership of the club, so my driving tasks continued for several more years. There were many times when I felt overworked and under-appreciated. It was particularly disheartening when the club attendance was poor. But over the years, the club produced an abundance of fruit by touching and changing the lives of hundreds of kids for God's glory. In addition, I enjoyed some recognition and reward when my involvement with the club enabled me to be on national radio with a congressman, as well as on local TV. I learned firsthand the truth behind First Peter 5:6 (NASB), which says, "Humble yourselves under the mighty hand of God, that He may exalt you at the proper   time."

I didn't know it at the time, but God was using my driving duties for the Bible Club to prepare me for the ministry I have today. I learned a lot from listening to those kids pour their hearts out to me each week. I spent extra time in prayer and Bible study each day, so that I could minister to them with the Word of God. It did my heart good to see what a difference it made in their lives. It still amazes me to think of how God used me to impact so many.

I certainly didn't have much to offer anyone. I had spent the last two decades raising children and keeping a home. I think there is a lot of truth to that statement which says, "God doesn't choose those who are able, but those who are available". All I did was offer myself to the Lord for His purposes, and it wasn't long before He took me up on my offer. First Corinthians 12:4-5 (NIV) says: "There are different kinds of gifts, but the same Spirit distributes them. There are different kinds of service, but the same Lord." If you've received Christ as your Savior, then you've been equipped to serve God and others for His glory. I guarantee that if you offer yourself and your God-given gifts to the Lord in all sincerity, He will show you how to put them to good use.

Jesus said that He did not come to be served, but to serve, and He expects us to have the same attitude. (Matthew 20:25-28) If the idea makes you fearful, I sympathize with you, because I have felt that way many times myself. God will help you overcome your fears if you ask Him to, and He's promised to provide you with all the strength you need to perform your tasks. (1 Peter 4:11)

If you are already in active service, know that the Lord has promised you reward and promotion as you persevere and remain faithful. (1 Corinthians 15:58; Matthew 25:23) Remember that there are no "insignificant" jobs in God's Kingdom. Every act of service we perform has great value in God's sight, even when we are not receiving thanks or recognition from others. Be encouraged by this precious promise from the Lord today: "God is not unjust; He will not forget your work and the love you have shown Him as you have helped His people and continue to help them." (Hebrews 6:10 NIV)

Lord, I thank You for equipping me to serve You and others. Today, I offer You all that I am, and all that I have, and I ask that You use me for Your glory. Give me a spirit of humility, so that I'll be willing to give myself to humble tasks. (Romans 12:16 AMP) Help me to always serve enthusiastically. (Romans 12:11 NLT) And encourage my heart when my efforts are unnoticed and unappreciated. Thank You that as I faithfully serve, You will be faithful to reward me!

Promise-Power Point: When I offer myself and my God-given gifts up to the Lord, I can expect Him to put me to work in His Kingdom, and to richly reward me for my service.

Divine Deals

"She is energetic, a hard worker, and watches for bargains." Proverbs 31:17-18 TLB

I once heard a godly man say that he prayed regularly, "Lord, make the best bargains come my way!" It inspired me so much that I began doing the same thing. When I read about the inspirational woman in Proverbs, and discovered that she had a habit of watching for bargains, I felt challenged by the Lord to not only pray for good bargains, but to eagerly search them out.

This was the case when my husband, Joe, and I needed a new dishwasher. Our old one just wasn't doing the job anymore, so we decided to go shopping for a new one. As we shopped, I felt impressed by the Lord to pray that we could also afford to buy a new dishwasher for our son, John, and his wife, Amy. They were expecting their son, William, and I knew in my heart that they could use an updated appliance like this to wash all the bottles and other baby things that they would be using on a regular basis. So I began earnestly praying that God would find us such an amazing deal on dishwashers, that we would be able to buy two at one time.

When Joe and I discovered how expensive these appliances had gotten since the last time we had bought one, we began to feel discouraged. Nevertheless, we continued to hope and pray that the Lord would send an extraordinary bargain our way. One day, Joe was reading one of our local newspapers and saw an advertisement for a fantastic sale on a high quality dishwasher with all kinds of options. The price was half of what we intended on spending on a single appliance, so we were able to buy two of them at an affordable price.

When Joe went to install John and Amy's new dishwasher, he found out why the Lord had enabled us to buy two of them, instead of just one. The kids' appliance had begun leaking water, and had the potential to do serious damage to their brand new kitchen floor.

You can't imagine what blessings you can reap until you begin asking God to send the best bargains your way. It's one of His ways of making your money go further, and of enabling you to be a greater blessing to others. So keep your eyes open, and keep a prayer on your lips. You might be surprised what you might find.

Lord, make me an effective and extraordinary bargain hunter. Show me where to look, and where to shop to get the best deals. Teach me to pray for the good buys I know You have for me, and help me to pray with the right motives. Make my money go a long way so that I can be a greater blessing to others. Today, I resolve to keep watching for bargains with eyes of faith!

Promise-Power Point: God wants me to get the most for my money, and He will lead me to the best bargains when I pray for them, and look for them, while relying on His guidance and grace.

Our "New Thing" God

"Forget the former things; do not dwell on the past. See, I am doing a new thing! Now it springs up; do you not perceive it?" Isaiah 43:18-19 NIV

When I was taking care of my little grandson, William, one day, I offered him a pretzel to snack on while I prepared his meal. He had his pacifier in his mouth at the time, and though he eagerly grabbed the pretzel from me, he refused to give up his pacifier. He began to whine and act miserable, and I told him that he couldn't have the pacifier and the pretzel at the same time – he had to give up one of them. Eventually, he chose the pretzel, and was able to enjoy every bite.

As I thought about all this, I realized that very often, the Lord is calling us to surrender something that we have, so that we can receive from Him something better that He is holding out to us. What are some of the things that can cause us to resist laying hold of the blessings the Lord offers us? Fear is one. We may think to ourselves, "What if I surrender what I have now, and end up with something inferior – or worse yet, nothing at all?" Habit is another. We become so accustomed to having something, or doing something a certain way, that we can't imagine something different. Procrastination can be an issue, too. We always think that we will do it – or deal with it – tomorrow, but we fail to realize that time is slipping away from us, and we are spending yet another day having to do without God's best for us. Stubbornness can also play a part. We would rather hold on to what we have than give up control and doing things our own way, not realizing or caring that we are only hurting ourselves. Worst of all, doubt and unbelief can be a factor. We don't fully trust God's intentions. We secretly think that He has ulterior motives, or that He doesn't really know or want what is best for us.

The truth is that our God is a "new thing" God. He is constantly challenging us to leave behind old things, so that we can receive the new opportunities, blessings, and rewards that He has for us. He says: "Forget the former things; do not dwell on the past. See, I am doing a new thing! Now it springs up; do you not perceive it?" (Isaiah 43:18-19 NIV) New things can be scary. We don't always like change, even change for the better. But in order for us to make progress in God's Kingdom, we must say goodbye to the "former things" that He is done with, before we can say hello to the new. The apostle Paul was well acquainted with this principle. Before he could enter in to the new life and calling God had for him, he had to leave behind his old way of life. We know from reading the Scriptures that the Lord was constantly calling Paul to a higher level of faith, obedience, and blessing. It wasn't easy for Paul, but it was rewarding. Today, you and I are still benefiting from the revelation knowledge that the Lord imparted to him. Paul wrote: "Brethren, I do not regard myself as having laid hold of it yet; but one thing I do: forgetting what lies behind and reaching forward to what lies ahead, I press on toward the goal for the prize of the upward call of God in Christ Jesus." (Philippians 3:13-14 NASB)

With God's help, you and I can also "press on" to lay hold of the new and better things that He has in store for us. As the Message Bible puts it: "Friends, don't get me wrong: By no means do I count myself an expert in all of this, but I've got my eye on the goal, where God is beckoning us onward – to Jesus. I'm off and running, and I'm not turning back"! (Philippians 3:13-14 MSG)

Lord, when You beckon me toward a higher level of obedience and blessing, help me not to resist You. Take away my fear of change, and help me to trust that You always want what is best for me. Thank You that as I press on to lay hold of the "new things" You have for me, I will enjoy greater blessings and draw others to You!

Promise-Power Point: As I seek God's wisdom and strength to leave behind all that the Lord calls me to, I can reach out and lay hold of the new and better plans, purposes, and opportunities He has for me.

Get Specific with Your Prayers

"Do not fret or have any anxiety about anything, but in every circumstance and in everything, by prayer and petition (definite requests), with thanksgiving, continue to make your wants known to God. And God's peace shall be yours..." Philippians 4:6-7 AMP

This past Christmas, my husband, Joe, and I were in the process of decorating our home, when we decided that we wanted to purchase some evergreen garland for our dining room. We began shopping at numerous department stores and self-improvement stores in our area. Everywhere we went, we found some sort of holiday garland, but either the appearance or the price didn't appeal to us. As we walked out of the third or fourth store, I sensed the Lord saying to my heart, "Tell Me exactly what kind of garland you'd like most. Be as specific as you can." Immediately, I silently began to pray. "Lord, I would like some lifelike evergreen garland with white lights, holly leaves, and red berries. Oh, and by the way, Lord, I'd like to get it at half price." The very next store my husband and I entered, we found the prettiest illuminated garland that we had ever seen. It not only had the exact lights, holly leaves, and berries that I had described, but it also had a beautiful snow effect that I hadn't even thought of asking for. It was breathtaking. And it was half price.

"Thank You, Lord," was all I could whisper at the time. I was so overwhelmed with how the God of the universe took an interest in such a small desire of my heart. And this wasn't the first time, either. Since I made a quality decision more than twenty years ago to get to know the Lord in a deeply personal way, I have discovered time and time again that He longs to be involved in the most intimate details of our lives.

It's true that we can ask God on a regular basis for the desires of our hearts – in a general sort of way. But I have found that when we make the effort to get specific with our prayer requests, the Lord is often willing to go to great lengths to reveal Himself to us through the answers He sends our way. Many times, when I am praying about something, I hear the same phrase that Jesus speaks often in the Gospels – "What do you want Me to do for you?" (Luke 18:41; Matthew 20:32; Mark 10:36; Mark 10:51) I know it's the Lord's way of saying, "Get specific with your requests." I believe that sometimes we can get lazy in our prayer life, especially when we've prayed for something over and over again. And I believe that it can grieve the heart of God. What would happen if we became more passionate in our praying? For one thing, we wouldn't have to settle for less than God's best. My Christmas garland is the perfect example. If I hadn't taken the time to describe to the Lord exactly what I wanted, I would have eventually just settled on some garland that would have made my house look nice and festive – but God wouldn't have used it to reveal Himself to me in a fresh, new way. And I would have missed out on that special moment of feeling wrapped in His matchless love.

The Bible says: "Do not fret or have any anxiety about anything, but in every circumstance and in everything, by prayer and petition (definite requests), with thanksgiving, continue to make your wants known to God." (Philippians 4:6 AMP) Don't miss the "definite requests" part of this verse. It shows that the Lord isn't afraid of you getting very specific with your requests. In fact, He welcomes it. Even though He knows your heart, He invites you to talk your needs and desires over with Him. He knows that it will draw you closer to Him, and it will open the door for Him to get more involved in every aspect of your life. David, the shepherd-king wrote: "The Lord directs the steps of the godly. He delights in every detail of their lives." (Psalm 37:23 NLT) Are you ready to go deeper with God, and to invite Him into every area of your life?

Lord, I confess that there have been times when I've been too casual with my prayers. Guard me from a lazy, half-hearted attitude when I am presenting my requests to You. Help me to take my conversation and communication with You more seriously. But remind me that nothing that concerns me is too trivial or insignificant for me to pray about. Thank You that as I put these principles into practice, I will have a more intimate, personal, and vibrant relationship with You!

Promise-Power Point: God challenges His people to be more specific and definite with their requests, and as I accept and rise to the challenge, He will reward me with untold blessings – the greatest of which is a closer relationship with Him.

The Power and Responsibility of Agreement

"And I will give you the keys of the Kingdom of Heaven. Whatever you forbid on earth will be forbidden in heaven, and whatever you permit on earth will be permitted in heaven." Matthew 16:19 NLT

When I had to have surgery to unblock my left tear duct, I had a negative reaction to the tubes the surgeon had placed in my eyelids. Because the symptoms of rejection were so severe, my doctor had to remove the tubes prematurely. Unfortunately, the lump that erupted on my left upper eyelid as a result of the tubes did not disappear after their removal. After receiving several treatments from two different doctors, the lump remained. One of my doctors suspected that the lump was cancerous, and he insisted that my surgeon do a biopsy. As I sat in his office waiting to be seen, I heard my surgeon speaking to another patient in the next room. As he described this woman's symptoms, and told her that she would need to be hospitalized and operated on to rule out cancer, my husband, Joe, turned to me and said, "That woman has the exact same problem that you do!" I confess that the similarities were uncanny, and for a moment, all I could feel was fear. Then, I got quiet in my spirit and sensed the Lord telling me not to agree with my husband's statement. In fact, He impressed upon me that I was to absolutely refuse the other woman's diagnosis as my own. I said to my husband, "I do NOT have the same problem that the other patient has." And I began to silently pray for God to intervene on my behalf in a mighty way, as I placed my trust in Him. When my surgeon finally came in to see me, he examined my eyelid and said that he didn't believe that my condition was serious, and that he could remove the lump right there in his office. When he did remove it, he took a biopsy of it, which proved to be negative for cancer.

As I pondered this experience later on, the Spirit of God brought to my remembrance Jesus' words in Matthew 18:19 (NLT): "If two of you agree here on earth concerning anything you ask, My Father in heaven will do it for you." This was the Lord's way of reminding me about the power of agreement. He warned me that it doesn't only act in positive ways, but it can act in negative ways, too. He revealed to me that if I had come into agreement with my husband's words of fear and doubt, it could have greatly hindered me from receiving God's best in the situation. You see, just as faith opens the door for God to work on our behalf, fear has the potential to open the door to satanic influence and involvement. So, when you and I are quick to receive and accept a negative report of some kind, we could be cutting ourselves off from the outcome that the Lord has in store for us. We must remember that just as God has plans for us – and they are always good – Satan, too, has plans for us – and they are always evil.

Right before Jesus talked about the power of agreement, He told His disciples: "I tell you the truth, whatever you forbid on earth will be forbidden in heaven, and whatever you permit on earth will be permitted in heaven." (Matthew 18:18 NLT) As followers of Christ, we have the power and privilege to "forbid" and "permit" certain things in the name of Jesus. We exercise this power and authority through our words, prayers, and actions. God expects us to use this power for good, and to direct it against the activities and schemes of the devil and his evil cohorts. To misdirect this power by using it to permit and call for things that are out of the will of God is an insult to Him, and it will have dire consequences.

The Lord wants to use you as an instrument and channel on this earth to bring about His will and purposes in people's lives and circumstances, including your own. So use your power of agreement carefully and prayerfully for the glory of God.

Lord, forgive me for the times that I neglected or misdirected the power and authority You have given me in this world. Teach me how to use this power properly and effectively so that I can partner with You to bring about Your highest purposes in lives and circumstances. Make me a devoted student of Your Word, so that I can have a working knowledge of Your will and Your truth. Today, I declare in agreement with Your Word, "Thy will be done on earth as it is in heaven!" (Matthew 6:10)

Promise-Power Point: As I use the awesome power of agreement in accordance with the plans and purposes of God, I will see Him move mightily to bring His will to pass.

I Still Have a Lot to Be Thankful For

"I will praise the Lord no matter what happens."
Psalm 34:1 TLB

When you and I suffer loss or disappointment, perspective is everything. The Lord made this fact clear to me in new ways, when He gave me a new strategy for responding to situations in which I don't get my own way. He told me to begin saying on a regular basis, "I still have a lot to be thankful for." It's a simple phrase, but it will change your life, if you allow it to change your perspective on things. Scripture tells us: "Thank [God] in everything [no matter what the circumstances may be; be thankful and give thanks], for this is the will of God for you [who are] in Christ Jesus." (1 Thessalonians 5:18 AMP) It's an insult to God when we focus on the things we've lost, rather than on the things we have left. And when we adopt a heartfelt "attitude of gratitude" in every situation, we experience levels of victory and power that lift us above our circumstances, and enable us to receive supernatural gifts from God.

So, practically speaking, what does saying, "I still have a lot to be thankful for," do? It guards us from grumbling and complaining. The Bible says that complaining opens the door to the Destroyer. (1 Corinthians 10:10-11) So refusing to grumble shuts the door on the enemy. It guards us from bitterness, resentment, unforgiveness, and offense – all attitudes that affect our fellowship with God, and greatly hinder our prayers. (Mark 11:24-25) It protects us from feeling sorry for ourselves. Pride is at the root of all self-pity, so when we refuse to feel sorry for ourselves, we are refusing to reap the penalty of a wrong response to our situation.

Saying, "I still have a lot to be thankful for," helps to keep our expectations of ourselves and others where they should be. And we are able to extend to them and ourselves the kind of mercy that heals, restores, and renews. Having an "attitude of gratitude" like this is powerful spiritual warfare. Every time we refuse ungodly attitudes and actions, and thank and praise God for all of the good in our lives, we neutralize the power of the dark forces, and we make ourselves a "hard target" for Satan, the enemy of our souls.

Scripture says: "Be thankful (appreciative), [giving praise to God always]." (Colossians 3:15 AMP) It's not easy to remain thankful in hurtful situations, and it often takes great faith to do so. But this kind of faith opens the door for God to bring great good out of our losses and disappointments, and to demonstrate His awesome power in our circumstances. If you are in a painful place today, look around you, and say to yourself and God, "I still have a lot to be thankful for!"

Lord, I know there have been times when I went through trials grumbling, complaining, and feeling bitter. Forgive me for feeling sorry for myself, and for imposing unrealistic expectations on others. Remind me that ungodly attitudes like these can give place to the enemy, and please strengthen me to resist them in the power of Your Spirit. Thank You, Lord, that no matter what happens, I still have a lot to be thankful for!

Promise-Power Point:** **As I refuse to give in to negative emotions in difficult times, I will position myself to receive rescue and relief from a grateful God.

God's Care in Times of Crisis

"The Lord is good, a refuge in times of trouble. He cares for those who trust in Him." Nahum 1:7 NIV

My family and I have experienced the Lord's mighty and tender loving care in times of crisis over the years, but never like we did when my husband, Joe, had a near-fatal heart attack. It was a Tuesday afternoon, when I was getting ready to keep a doctor's appointment that I had made weeks beforehand to follow up on some health issues I had been dealing with. Even though it was a weekday, my husband was at home because he had lost his job months earlier, and was still unemployed. As I prepared to walk out the door, Joe came to me and told me that he was having some discomfort in his chest area, so I insisted that he take the 2:15 appointment that I had with our doctor that day. When our doctor ran some preliminary tests on Joe, he couldn't find anything seriously wrong with him, but he still insisted that I drive him to the hospital right away.

By the time we arrived at the hospital, my husband's pain was getting worse, and more tests were conducted to find out what the problem was. As it turned out, my husband had a massive heart attack as he was hooked up to monitors that confirmed that fact to the hospital staff. Suddenly, the room was filled with doctors and technicians, and before I knew it, Joe was whisked away from me, to a room where some exploratory surgery could be done. A kindly social worker led me to a waiting room where I could wait for updates on my husband's condition.

As I waited, prayed, and made phone calls to my children and other family members, some of the hospital staff noticed that my face was unnaturally red. They insisted on taking my blood pressure, and when they discovered that it was dangerously high, they called my doctor, who recommended that I be taken to the emergency room. I remember telling them, "My husband's having a heart attack! I can't leave him now!" I desperately prayed for God's help, and as I did, the social worker asked if I had any medication on me that would help to reduce my blood pressure. When I said that I had some at home, she suggested that I call my son and ask him to pick it up for me. As I was discussing the matter on the phone with my son, a lady sitting across from me in the waiting room said that she was on the very same medication, in the same dosage, and she would be more than happy to give it to me. As I turned to the social worker for her approval, she smiled and said, "Yes, by all means, take it!" And I marveled at how the Lord made a way for me to remain nearby for my husband in his time of need.

Finally, I was ushered into a recovery room where Joe was left to recover from some minor heart surgery. I kissed him and held his hand, and I thanked God for His loving care. A nurse apologized that they had no available beds in the medical intensive care unit, so they were going to have to place my husband in the surgical ICU, instead. All of a sudden, it dawned on me that this was the unit that my son, John's, wife worked in, and Joe and I rejoiced that "Nurse Amy" would be close by during his recovery.

My husband's doctors were amazed at his "miraculous" recovery, and he was released from the hospital only 48 hours after his heart attack. One of the doctors told Joe, "You had everything working in your favor," and it was true. God had seen that I had a doctor's appointment scheduled for almost the exact time that Joe began having chest pains. And we found out later that the best possible doctor my husband could have had was on call at the hospital that day. The Lord had made provision for my own health needs by causing the woman with the medication to be nearby when I needed her. And He made sure that no beds were available in the regular ICU, so that Joe would be placed under our daughter-in-law's watchful eye.

The Bible says: "The Lord is good, a refuge in times of trouble. He cares for those who trust in Him." (Nahum 1:7 NIV) When my husband's health and life were threatened that day, I decided to put my trust in the living God, and His ability and willingness to care for us in our crisis. As a result, He revealed His presence, power, and provision in a way that amazes us to this day. The next time you are in a crisis of your own, open the door to God's loving and mighty care by placing your wholehearted trust in Him!

Lord, I praise You for being a God who deeply cares for Your devoted ones. Teach me how to cooperate with You to increase my faith in You and Your Word. Don't let me live my life doubting Your love, Your power, or Your provision. Thank You that as I turn to You first in times of trouble, and put my trust in You, I will experience the support and care that only You can give!

Promise-Power Point: God will reveal His awesome power on my behalf when I believe in His love and goodness, and put my trust in Him.

The Power of Positive Speech

"Words kill, words give life; they're either poison or fruit – you choose." Proverbs 18:21 MSG

My husband, Joe, and I have been raising pet ducks for many years, and we've had our male duck, Larry, for 14 of those years. Every molting season, Larry would lose all of his brightly-colored, iridescent feathers, and for a time, he'd look woefully scraggly. He would hang his head low, and he'd not only lose his feathers, but also his confidence, boldness, and dignity. The older Larry got, the harder the molting process would be on his health and morale. Seeing our little man so depressed prompted me to ask the Lord what we could do to ease Larry's pain and discouragement. That's when the Holy Spirit brought to my remembrance Proverbs 18:21 (NIV): "The tongue has the power of life and death, and those who love it will eat its fruit."

Suddenly, I knew exactly what we needed to do. I told my husband that we were going to be very careful about how we spoke around Larry while he was looking so shabby. Instead of saying, "Wow, Larry, you really look ratty!" we were going to say, "What beautiful new feathers you're getting, Larry!" We replaced all of our negative speech around Larry with compliments and affirmations, and we kept encouraging him and reassuring him. No doubt, Larry could tell by just the inflections in our voices that we were speaking highly of him, instead of commenting on his dreadful appearance.

I must tell you that changing our attitudes and words toward Larry each time he goes through the molting process has made all the difference. His head no longer hangs low, and he walks just as proudly as when he has his full, beautifully-colored plumage the rest of the year. This experiment has taught my husband and me a memorable lesson about the power of our words, and we have a newfound appreciation for the importance of our speech, and how it can profoundly affect others, as well as ourselves.

Imagine the difference you and I could make in the lives of our spouses, children, grandchildren, parents, siblings, coworkers, neighbors, and others, if we would simply be more aware of our words, and more considerate with our speech. Can you think of someone who could benefit from your positive speech today?

Lord, it grieves my heart to think of all the times I spoke harmful words to others, instead of words that heal. Give me revelation knowledge about the true power of my speech and conversation, and do it in a way that will impact my mind and my heart. Whenever I am tempted to speak rashly or thoughtlessly, remind me that when I sow seeds of hurtful speech, I could very well reap a harvest of pain and regret. Today, I commit to seeking and relying on Your wisdom and strength to speak words that build up, instead of tear down!

Promise-Power Point: As I remind myself often that my words have tremendous power and authority on this earth, and as I work with the Lord to measure them before I open my mouth, I will impact others for their good, and for the glory of God.

Responding to Rebels

"He will even deliver the one [for whom you intercede] who is not innocent; yes, he will be delivered through the cleanness of your hands." Job 22:30 AMP

I recently heard a powerful and encouraging teaching about how we can make a real difference in people's lives, even when they are living in blatant rebellion against God. Sometimes, the Lord instructs us to love these people from a distance. But other times, these rebellious people will be our own loved ones who God expects us to remain in close relationship with. They may be our spouses, our children, our parents, or our siblings. And even though their ungodly behavior may deeply hurt us, the Lord expects us to follow His lead in impacting their lives for good.

First, we must keep the lines of communication open. Have you ever given anyone the silent treatment? I used to be so good at employing this subtle form of revenge that I elevated it to an art form. That was until the Lord led me to a verse in Scripture that pierced my soul with conviction, and changed my heart and life. Jesus said, "So be merciful (sympathetic, tender, responsive, and compassionate) even as your Father is [all these]." (Luke 6:36 AMP) The word, "responsive," was the one that struck me the hardest. No more building walls between me and those who hurt me, or who didn't meet my unreasonable expectations. I was commanded by the Master Himself to demonstrate the God-kind of love to others in my character, conduct, and conversation. By doing this, we leave the door open for the Lord to use us as His instruments to influence those around us who need a touch from God.

Second, we must continue praying and interceding for these difficult people, even when it seems that our prayers are going unanswered. No more getting discouraged when we're not getting the results from our prayers that we expect. No more quitting and giving up just because God isn't working fast enough to suit us. No more throwing our hands up in exasperation because we feel like our time and energy are too important to waste on people who might never see the light. Romans 12:12 (MSG) says, "Don't quit in hard times; pray all the harder." From now on, when you and I even THINK about letting up on our petitions before the throne, we will declare out loud, "I have only begun to fight!" And we will cling to God's holy promise which says, "The earnest prayer of a righteous person has great power and produces wonderful results." (James 5:16 NLT)

Third, we must remind ourselves that the battle is the Lord's, and that our part is to pray and stand firm in our faith. As a mere youth, David defeated a giant because he had gotten the revelation that it wasn't his might that would give him victory, but the Lord's. He boldly declared to Goliath and his troops: "All those gathered here will know that it is not by sword or spear that the Lord saves; for the battle is the Lord's, and He will give all of you into our hands." (1 Samuel 17:47 NIV) Because David relied on God's power to defeat the enemy, he emerged victorious. And you and I will gain the victory over the forces of evil coming against our loved ones, when we fight the battle in prayer, relying on God's Spirit to empower and direct us. Is there a rebel in YOUR life right now who could benefit from your heeding this message and putting it into practice?

Lord, I'm so grateful that You have equipped me to make a difference in the lives of those who are resisting Your will for them. Fill me with a holy determination to persist in prayer for these people, and to love them with Your kind of love. Guard me from discouragement and doubt, and remind me that the battle belongs to You. Thank You for all of the hearts that will be eternally transformed as I put Your life-changing principles to work!

Promise-Power Point: I have God-given power and authority to be a world-changer for Christ, and as I follow His battle plan and demonstrate His kind of love, He will use me to draw others to Him for all eternity.

God's Greater Power

"Be strong and courageous! Don't be afraid or discouraged because of the king of Assyria or his mighty army, for there is a power far greater on our side!" 2 Chronicles 32:7,8 NLT

The Bible tells us that there will be times when heartache and hardship come our way, even though we have been serving the Lord wholeheartedly. This was the case with good King Hezekiah of Judah in Chapter 32 of Second Chronicles. Scripture says: "After all that Hezekiah had so faithfully done, Sennacherib king of Assyria came and invaded Judah." (2 Chronicles 32:1 NIV) When we face adversity, it's always a good idea to ask the Lord if we have contributed to our troubles in any way. But we must keep in mind that sometimes we will come under attack because we are following God's plan for us, and Satan isn't happy about it.

With the whole Assyrian army coming against the people of Judah, Hezekiah wisely chooses to put his trust in the Lord. He tells his people: "Be strong and courageous! Don't be afraid or discouraged because of the king of Assyria or his mighty army, for there is a power far greater on our side! He may have a great army, but they are merely men. We have the Lord our God to help us and to fight our battles for us!" (2 Chronicles 32:7-8 NLT) When you and I come under attack, if we will commit the battle to the Lord, and recognize that the greater power is on our side, we will find peace and reassurance in the midst of the storm.

By insulting God and threatening His people, Sennacherib hopes to disarm and dishearten the people of Judah and their king. He says: "What makes you think your God can rescue you from me? I say it again — no god of any nation or kingdom has ever yet been able to rescue his people from me or my ancestors. How much less will your God rescue you from my power!" (v. 14-15 NLT) When you and I are going through trials, Satan will try to get us to focus on those around us who have fallen and failed as a result of his relentless onslaught. If we are wise, we will claim God's promises of protection and victory, such as Psalm 91:7 (NIV) which says, "A thousand may fall at your side, ten thousand at your right hand, but it will not come near you."

As the battle heats up, Hezekiah recognizes his need for strength and reassurance, and he cries out to God for help. "Then King Hezekiah and the prophet Isaiah son of Amoz cried out in prayer to God in heaven." (v. 20 NLT) The next verse reveals God's response to the faith and prayers of His servant Hezekiah. "And the Lord sent an angel who destroyed the Assyrian army with all its commanders and officers. So Sennacherib was forced to return home in disgrace to his own land. And when he entered the temple of his god, some of his own sons killed him there with a sword." (v. 21 NLT) Just as the Lord executed a swift and decisive victory for His people in this Bible account, you and I can count on Him to fight for us when we cooperate with His battle plan. Always remember – the greater power is on our side!

Lord, whenever I am feeling attacked or put down in any way, help me to turn to You first. Remind me often that even the devil himself and all of his evil forces are no match for You. Don't let others' failures and defeats cause my faith in You to falter or fail. Grant me Your perspective on every challenge and trial that comes my way. Thank You that as I let You fight my battles, I will have all the help of Heaven on my side!

Promise-Power Point: When I come under attack in any way, if I will cry out to God and commit the battle to Him, He will cause me to come out on top, no matter how great the odds are against me.

Better to Trust the Lord

"It is better to trust the Lord than to put confidence in people." Psalm 118:8 NLT

When my husband, Joe, began having severe pain in his neck, it got so bad that it gave him pounding headaches, and made his blood pressure rise alarmingly. When he went to see his doctor, a large growth was discovered in his neck. Two more doctors confirmed the presence of the growth through various medical tests. All of the doctors suspected cancer, and a specialist told Joe that his chances of having it were 90%. A biopsy was ordered, but could not be performed for at least three weeks. Joe and I both dreaded having to wait that long to get the proper diagnosis and treatment. My husband was suffering terribly, and it grieved me to see him in so much pain. Because of that, I made a decision. I decided that I was not going to wait on doctors to heal my husband. I was going to wait on God.

I began praying for Joe's healing like never before. I started tucking him in bed at night, and praying aloud over him, asking the Lord to heal him before his test date even arrived. I reminded God over and over that we were not waiting on doctors for Joe's healing, but we were waiting on Him. At one point, Joe told me, "One thing is for certain — I'm not getting out of this without surgery." He had heard the doctors' reports about the growth in his neck. Three different doctors had felt it, and it was confirmed by ultrasound tests. I knew I couldn't afford to have the same mindset that Joe had. God was challenging me to believe Him for greater things. And it was God's Word and promises that bolstered my faith. David wrote: "Some trust in chariots and some in horses, but we trust in the name of the Lord our God." (Psalm 20:7 NIV) The Holy Spirit brought this verse to my remembrance, and urged me not to put my confidence in doctors, but in God. The Lord could certainly use doctors as part of my husband's healing process, but I was not to put my faith in them, or to wait on them for help. As I prayed for Joe as though God was our only hope, we began to see some real improvements in his symptoms. The pain lessened. The swelling went down. Joe was no longer incapacitated, but was able to function normally. And we began to thank and praise God that His healing power was already at work in my husband's body.

Psalm 60:11-12 (NIV) says: "Give us aid against the enemy, for the help of man is worthless. With God we will gain the victory, and He will trample down our enemies." These words of David's kept coming to mind during this time, and I began praying them in faith whenever I was tempted to doubt. I confess there were times when I would hear the doctors' negative reports in my ears, and fear would start to rise in my heart. Then I would remind myself that Scripture instructs us to think only on "whatever things are of good report," and I would "cast down" those thoughts that did not agree with God's Word. (Philippians 4:8 NKJV; 2 Corinthians 10:5 KJV) A good doctor can be a Godsend. And the Lord can, and often does, use doctors to heal us. But if we wait solely upon the medical profession for help, we could be waiting a very long time, often with very disappointing results to show for it. While the "help of man" can truly prove "worthless" at times, the help of God never will.

When the day finally came for Joe's biopsy, no growth could be found in his neck. The same type of medical tests that confirmed the growth's existence, confirmed its absence. And all final reports showed absolutely no cancer. The doctors can explain it any way they want to, but my family and I know that it was the hand of God that healed my husband, and we are giving Him all the glory. We have learned firsthand the truth of His Word – "It is better to trust the Lord than to put confidence in people." (Psalm 118:8 NLT)

Lord, help me to never misplace my confidence, but to keep my faith in You at all times. Give me a revelation of Your matchless power and love that will move me to trust in You alone from now on. Thank You that as I depend on You for all my needs, I will experience Your supernatural protection and provision!

Promise-Power Point: When I seek God first in times of adversity, and keep my expectations in Him, He will show Himself strong on my behalf, and rescue me and mine.

The Recipe for Abundant Joy

"Ask, using My name, and you will receive, and you will have abundant joy." John 16:24 NLT

My toddler grandson, William, loves to draw, so I often lend him some of my mechanical pencils, which seem to be his favorites. On one particular occasion, the pencil he was using ran out of lead, and he began shaking it in frustration. I told him, "Come here, and I will put new leads in your pencil so you can keep drawing." I was busy in the kitchen at the time, and when Will refused to come to me for help, I forgot all about it. The following morning, I found that empty mechanical pencil and I stared at it, thinking about what transpired the day before. Suddenly, I felt a pain in my heart. If my grandson had only come to me for help, I would have supplied him with all the leads he wanted, and I would have rejoiced at seeing the look of joy on his face. Instead, out of ignorance or stubbornness, he neglected to ask for my help, and he had to do without. That's when I got a revelation. How many times has the Lord desperately wanted to help His children, and to provide for them when they had a need or desire, and for whatever reason, they refused or didn't bother to go to Him?

I thought of Jesus' promise in John 16:24 (NLT), which says, "Ask, using My name, and you will receive, and you will have abundant joy." Talk about an invitation. The King of Kings Himself pleads with His followers to come to Him with their requests, simply so that they can experience the joy of answered prayer, and so that He can bask in their gladness and gratitude. Since I began wholeheartedly devoting myself to the Lord twenty-plus years ago, and studying His teachings in-depth, I've become a world-class "asker". If you spend any time in the Scriptures, it doesn't take long for you to realize how many times the Savior says, "Ask!" The thing that touches my heart most is that the Creator of the universe is not just making a suggestion to His followers, but a heartfelt plea. He knows that asking can make the difference between success and failure, sickness and health, poverty and abundance, and even life and death.

Frankly, I am stunned and dismayed at how many Christians fail to go to God first with their needs and desires. In some cases, they've gone first to friends, family members, or coworkers. Or doctors or banks. These can all be good things, and God can certainly use them to help us, but they should never be our first resort. When we need help of any kind, we should go to the throne, before we go to the phone.

If there were an "asking meter" in heaven, how would you register on it? How about your joy level? Could you be missing out on the "abundant joy" that Christ promises, simply because you don't "ask and receive" as much as you should? Remember the Bible's solemn admonition to you today – "You don't have what you want because you don't ASK God for it." (James 4:2 NLT)

Lord, I am so grateful that You want me to ask for Your help, Your healing, and Your provision when I need or desire them. Renew my mind and heart so that I will see You as You really are – a too-good-to-be-true God, who desires to bless His children and make their joy overflow. Today, I make a quality decision to begin asking You to supply all my needs, and to give me the desires of my heart, as I give You first place in my life!

Promise-Power Point: God has invited me to ask Him for the things I need and desire, but it's up to me to take Him up on His offer, so that I can experience the fullness of His blessings, and His abundant joy.

Consider Him Faithful

"And by faith even Sarah, who was past childbearing age, was enabled to bear children because she considered Him faithful who had made the promise."
Hebrews 11:11 NIV

When we are going through trials – especially severe and prolonged ones – it can be tempting to give in to doubt and discouragement. But if we remember that a lack of faith can rob us of God's best, we can cooperate with Him to resist weakening and wavering in our belief. One way we can do that is to study how God's people in the Bible stood firm in difficult times, and received the miracles that He had for them.

When I was going through a very long trial of my own, I sought the Lord about how I could stabilize my wavering faith, which I knew wasn't helping my situation. He led me to Hebrews 11:11 (NIV), which says: "By faith even Sarah, who was past childbearing age, was enabled to bear children because she considered Him faithful who had made the promise." The words, "she considered Him faithful" came alive in my spirit, and I began to understand what the Lord was saying to me. If I would make a quality decision to believe that God was indeed faithful – to His character, His Word, and His promises – my faith would hold steady so that I could receive the blessings and rewards He had in store for me.

The Bible makes it clear that Sarah's situation looked hopeless. She was well past the age of childbearing, and yet God had promised her and Abraham a child of their own. To her credit, "she considered [God] Who had given her the promise to be reliable and trustworthy and true to His word." (Hebrews 11:11 AMP) And as a result, she saw the fulfillment of His promise to her. Jesus' mother, Mary, is another woman in the Bible who can provide us with inspiration in this area. An angel from the Lord told her that she would give birth to a son, even though she had never been intimate with a man. And yet, the Scriptures say of her, "Blessed is she who has believed that the Lord would fulfill His promises to her!" (Luke 1:45 NIV) In other words, she considered God faithful – and became the mother of the promised Messiah.

I don't know what difficulties or heartaches you may be facing right now, but I can tell you this: If you will trust in the faithfulness of God, you will see Him move heaven and earth to bring His very best purposes to pass in your life. Today, join with me in declaring – *"I refuse to doubt my God!"*

Lord, I regret the times I missed out on Your best for me because I doubted Your goodness, Your wisdom, and Your Word. Help me to cooperate with You for the building of my faith through personal worship, prayer, and Bible study, so that I can stand firm in the most difficult of times. Remind me of inspiring biblical accounts like Sarah's and Mary's so that I won't yield to unbelief in tests and trials. Today, I purpose in my heart to consider You faithful, Lord!

Promise-Power Point: **When I take God at His Word and consider Him reliable and trustworthy, He will reveal His awesome power and provision on my behalf.**

How Anger Harms

"Cease from anger, and forsake wrath; Do not fret – it only causes harm." Psalm 37:8 NKJV

When my husband, Joe, came home from the hospital after his open-heart surgery, he brought with him some materials that were designed to help him protect his heart and his health. As I looked over his paperwork one day, I noticed a questionnaire asking heart patients how they respond to various situations. The idea was to help these patients to recognize any behaviors or habits that might be harming their health. I couldn't help noticing that the very first unhealthy response listed was anger. I had been telling my husband for years that his short temper wasn't good for him, but here I was seeing in black and white just how right I was. Then, some weeks later, I was listening to a powerful message from a well-respected man of God who said that anger is a form of suicide. Can anger kill? I believe it can. Sometimes, it kills slowly, causing sickness, disease, and pain in the body. And sometimes it kills quickly, causing sudden heart attacks and strokes. My husband had already had one heart attack, and I knew that his negative emotions and attitudes were major factors – and he knew it, too. The Bible says: "A calm and undisturbed mind and heart are the life and health of the body, but envy, jealousy, and wrath are like rottenness of the bones." (Proverbs

14:30 AMP) There's no getting away from it — our emotions and attitudes have an impact on our health, and even our lifespan. As the New Living Translation says, "A relaxed attitude lengthens life." (Proverbs 14:30 NLT)

One of the reasons why anger is so destructive is that it makes us vulnerable to satanic attack. Scripture says: "Don't sin by letting anger control you. Don't let the sun go down while you are still angry, for anger gives a foothold to the devil." (Ephesians 4:26-27 NLT) When we fail to control our temper, we move out from under God's umbrella of protection, and we become easy targets for the forces of darkness. Years ago, I had a car accident right after I had prayed for protection for myself and my children. I confess that my faith had been shaken, and I sought the Lord about the matter, and asked Him what went wrong. He pointed out that right before the accident, I had been yelling at my children, and I had opened a door in the spirit realm to Satan, who "comes only to steal and kill and destroy," as Jesus said. (John 10:10 NIV) It was a costly lesson to learn, but also a very valuable one.

The Bible tells us: "Let every man be quick to hear [a ready listener], slow to speak, slow to take offense and to get angry. For man's anger does not promote the righteousness God [wishes and requires]." (James 1:19-20 AMP) We simply cannot please God when we have a tendency to lose our tempers easily. Patience is a fruit of the Holy Spirit (Galatians 5:22), and with God's help, we can develop that fruit more and more, so that we can be Christlike examples to the world. The apostle Paul wrote: "Get rid of all bitterness, rage and anger, brawling and slander, along with every form of malice. Be kind and compassionate to one another, forgiving each other, just as in Christ God forgave you." (Ephesians 4:31-32 NIV) When we get a revelation of how much the Lord has forgiven us, we will be more likely to walk in forgiveness toward others. Then the devil will have a very difficult time attacking or defeating us.

King David wisely wrote: "Stop being angry! Turn from your rage! Do not lose your temper – it only leads to harm." (Psalm 37:8 NLT) Your anger does have the potential to harm others, but mostly, it will harm YOU. As Ecclesiastes 7:9 (MSG) says, "Don't be quick to fly off the handle. Anger boomerangs. You can spot a fool by the lumps on his head."

Lord, Your Word makes it clear that when I lose my temper easily, I could be harming myself and my witness. Make me a peaceful and patient person. Show me how to fully cooperate with You to that end. Help me to forgive others quickly and thoroughly, the way You do. Thank You that my obedience in this area will enable You to bless me and use me in greater ways than ever before!

Promise-Power Point: Uncontrolled anger is not God's will for me because it can destroy my health and my relationships, and as I purpose to demonstrate patience and peace, I will live a longer and happier life.

How We Can Touch God

"And wherever He went – into villages, towns or countryside – they placed the sick in the marketplaces. They begged Him to let them touch even the edge of His cloak, and all who touched Him were healed." Mark 6:56 NIV

These words are some of the most comforting in all of Scripture for me.   Countless times, I have needed healing for my body, my mind, or my emotions, and have desperately wanted to reach out and touch the Lord, and be touched by Him, and these words have reassured me that this is a real possibility.   We know that it is our faith that enables us to reach out and touch God.   But what are some practical ways that we can exercise and release our faith for this very purpose?

We can touch God through our prayers.   Jesus said that when we join our prayers with others, we can know that He is in our midst. (Matthew 18:19-20)   But we must not think that we can't be totally alone with God to reach out to Him.   The Savior also said, "But when you pray, go away by yourself, shut the door behind you, and pray to your Father in private.   Then your Father, who sees everything, will reward you." (Matthew 6:6 NLT)   God's rewards can include healing, protection, or provision – as well as wisdom, joy, and peace.   Our God is not a distant God.   When Jesus said that He would always be with His followers, He meant it.   I like the way the Amplified Bible brings out the true meaning of the Lord's heartfelt statement: "Behold, I am with you all the days (perpetually, uniformly, and on every occasion), to the [very] close and consummation of the age. Amen (so let it be)." (Matthew 28:20 AMP) You and I have the privilege of calling on God every moment of every day, and that is a privilege that we should constantly take advantage of, as we live our lives in an often cold and hostile world.

We can also touch God through our praise, thanksgiving, and worship. Psalm 22:3 (KJV) says that God inhabits the praises of His people. That means that the Lord has a way of showing up and showing off in our situation when we are inclined to resist grumbling and complaining, and we instead lift our hearts in praise to Him. Psalm 89:15 (NLT) says: "Happy are those who hear the joyful call to worship, for they will walk in the light of Your presence, Lord." When God reveals Himself to us, and in our circumstance, light comes on the scene, and darkness has to flee. Satan and his evil forces cannot stand against the presence and power of God. Psalm 8:2 (AMP) reassures us that our praises have the ability to "silence the enemy and the avenger". So we can think of praise and worship as effective spiritual warfare.

Another way we can touch God is by believing and obeying the Word of God. Many years ago, when I was desperate to have the Lord reveal Himself to me in life-changing ways, He told me, "You will find Me in My Word." That's when I began diligently reading and studying the Scriptures. As I applied their principles to every area of my life, and claimed the promises therein, God began making Himself real to me more and more. One promise that I claimed often was John 14:21 (AMP): "The person who has My commands and keeps them is the one who [really] loves Me; and whoever [really] loves Me will be loved by My Father, and I [too] will love him and will show (reveal, manifest) Myself to him. [I will let Myself be clearly seen by him and make Myself real to him.]" Think of it: The Son of God Himself will allow us to see Him clearly when we believe, love, and obey Him.

If you have trusted Christ as your Savior, then you have the power to touch God, and to be touched by Him. What are you waiting for?

Lord, I praise You for making a way for me to have an intensely personal and vibrant relationship with You. Teach Me how to use every resource that You have made available to me, so that I can be as close to You as You want me to be. Don't ever let me be satisfied with having a shallow or superficial relationship with You. Thank You for helping me to know You, love You, and serve You the way You desire and deserve!

Promise-Power Point: God has given me the ability and privilege to reach out and touch Him through prayer, praise, and obedience to His Word.

Blessings We Don't Deserve

"He does not treat us as our sins deserve or repay us according to our iniquities." Psalm 103:10 NIV

I was taking care of my grandson, William, in my home recently, when I decided to give him a bath. As I turned on the bath faucet, only cold water came out. "Oh, no! I thought. Of all times for us to be out of hot water!" As I turned to the Lord in prayer, my mind suddenly became filled with thoughts of condemnation. I began thinking about all of the ways I had failed God recently, and how I didn't deserve His help. As cold water continued to run from the bath faucet, the Holy Spirit brought to my remembrance God's promise in Psalm 103: "He does not treat us as our sins deserve or repay us according to our iniquities." (Psalm 103:10 NIV) Immediately, I gained the courage to go to God in prayer. "Lord, Your Word says that You don't treat us as our sins deserve, and on the basis of Your Word, I'm asking You to promptly restore our hot water so that I can give my grandson a bath." A few moments later, I checked our water again, and there was more than enough hot water to give William his bath. I praised and thanked God with all my heart, grateful that I took God at His Word, and had the courage to ask for His help.

It's true that our God is a God of mercy. But it's also true that He's a God of justice. He takes sin so seriously that He gave His own Son over to a gruesome death, so that you and I could have a personal and intimate relationship with Him, a holy God. When we enter into that relationship by accepting Christ's sacrifice as payment for our sins, then we become heirs of His "very great and precious promises" (2 Peter 1:4 NIV) – even His promise which says that "He does not treat us as our sins deserve".

The Bible says: "If we [freely] admit that we have sinned and confess our sins, He is faithful and just (true to His own nature and promises) and will forgive our sins [dismiss our lawlessness] and [continuously] cleanse us from all unrighteousness [everything not in conformity to His will in purpose, thought, and action]." (1 John 1:9 AMP) This is how we, as believers, should deal with our sin on a regular basis, so that we can walk closely with our Lord every day – hearing from Him clearly, and having Him hear us.

Don't take sin lightly, but don't put up with the devil's condemnation, either. When you are in need, don't hesitate to turn to the Lord in prayer, claiming His eternal promise that He won't treat you as your sins deserve.

Lord, thank You that Your Word says, "There is now no condemnation for those who are in Christ Jesus". (Romans 8:1) Remind me often that it is Satan who is "the accuser" of Your followers (Revelation 12:10), and teach me how to stand firm against his every attack. Today, I commit to being quick to confess my sins to You, and to receive the forgiveness and cleansing You have promised me!

Promise-Power Point: God will not treat me as my sins deserve, because I am living my life for Him, and claiming His promises of forgiveness and favor.

Peace of Mind and Heart

"We have the mind of Christ (the Messiah) and do hold the thoughts (feelings and purposes) of His heart."
1 Corinthians 2:16 AMP

One of the things that most people in this world are searching for on a regular basis is peace of mind and heart. Our generation is surrounded by more noise, activity, and busyness than ever before, and these things are stealing our peace. Jesus talked about peace a lot because He knew how important it was to our well-being and our purpose in life. In fact, before He went to the Cross, He told His followers, "I am leaving you with a gift – peace of mind and heart! And the peace I give isn't fragile like the peace the world gives. So don't be troubled or afraid." (John 14:27 TLB) Isn't it interesting that one of the most precious gifts the Savior chose to leave His loved ones was His own kind of peace?

If you are looking for more peace of mind and heart today, I have some words of encouragement for you, taken right from the Scriptures. First Corinthians 2:16 (NIV) says: "We have the mind of Christ." In other words, once we accept Christ as our Savior and Lord, we have the potential to think the way He does. The Amplified translation says it this way: "We have the mind of Christ (the Messiah) and do hold the thoughts (feelings and purposes) of His heart." (1 Corinthians

2:16 AMP) Notice that I used the word, "potential". That's because thinking like Christ is something that needs to be developed. As we walk in close fellowship with the Lord on a daily basis, His Spirit in us is constantly working with us to "reprogram" our minds and our thought processes. The best way to speed up our progress in this area is to renew our minds with the Word of God, which not only teaches us about God's truths, but it also reveals the world's lies.

The Bible says: "A calm and undisturbed mind and heart are the life and health of the body." (Proverbs 14:30 AMP) Our thought life can greatly affect, not only our peace, but the health of our bodies. And our physical health can greatly affect how much God can use us to make a difference in this world. Prayer can be a powerful weapon in laying hold of the supernatural peace that is our inheritance in Christ. The apostle Paul wrote: "Do not be anxious about anything, but in every situation, by prayer and petition, with thanksgiving, present your requests to God. And the peace of God, which transcends all understanding, will guard your hearts and your minds in Christ Jesus." (Philippians 4:6-7 NIV) Anything worth worrying about, is worth praying about. Years ago, I heard someone say, "Those things you are concerned about today – have you prayed about them as much as you have worried about them?" The next verse in this passage by Paul reveals an essential key to walking in God's peace. "Finally, brothers and sisters, whatever is true, whatever is noble, whatever is right, whatever is pure, whatever is lovely, whatever is admirable – if anything is excellent or praiseworthy – think about such things." (Philippians 4:8 NIV) Those thoughts that don't line up with these scriptural standards should be "cast down" and eliminated from our minds swiftly and soundly. (2 Corinthians 10:3-6 NKJV)

When negative thoughts of any kind assail my mind, I answer them back with, "I'm not having those thoughts. Jesus doesn't think like that, and neither do I!" If I am alone, I might declare it out loud. If I'm in the presence of others, I speak it to myself within my thoughts. The idea is to promptly reject wrong thoughts so that they don't take root in my mind and heart, and become a stronghold that acts like a deadly poison in my soul. We may not always be able to prevent negative thoughts from entering our minds, but we can certainly refuse to dwell on them. God's Word makes it clear that you and I have the ability, and the responsibility, to monitor our thoughts. Today, are you ready to begin claiming the mind of Christ, and the supernatural peace that are your rightful inheritance? Then start thinking about what you're thinking about, and take control of your thought life!

Lord, thank You that I don't have to put up with negative and ungodly thoughts that can steal my peace and health. Help me to cooperate with Your Holy Spirit for the renewing of my mind. Remind me to accelerate my progress by spending regular time alone with You and Your Word. Teach me how to refuse thoughts and ideas that contradict Your truth. Today, I claim the mind of Christ that makes me the overcomer You have called me to be!

Promise-Power Point: As I exercise my God-given ability to monitor and control my thought life, I will experience the peace that transcends all understanding.

Realize Your Hopes and Dreams

"We want each of you to show this same diligence to the very end, so that what you hope for may be fully realized." Hebrews 6:11 NIV

I was looking through an old journal of mine recently, and I stumbled upon a page where I described how discouraged I was over the seemingly nonexistent growth of my ministry. My heart ached as I read the words that must have been difficult for me to write. I was obviously weary and disheartened at the time, and I talked about wanting to quit. When I looked at the date on my journal entry, I shuddered. It was less than two years before I published my first book. I began to think about the tens of thousands of readers I never would have reached with the love and truth of God, if I had quit and given up during those early days of my ministry.

The Lord led me to this journal entry for the very purpose of encouraging my heart. Once again, I was feeling as though my ministry was at a standstill, and that perhaps it was time for me to lay it down. He drove His point home when He showed me the verse above in Hebrews 6:11. If I was to "fully realize" the things I hoped for – including fulfilling my God-given purpose and potential – then I was going to have to remain diligent "to the very end".

Too often, Christians are given an assignment from God, and start out laboring for the Lord with great enthusiasm. But after they have invested much time and effort with little to show for it, they quit before they realize their hopes and dreams. Proverbs 13:4 (NIV) says: "The sluggard craves and gets nothing, but the desires of the diligent are fully satisfied." Another word for diligent is "persistent". In other words, when God gives us an assignment, we don't quit until He tells us to quit. If we're not receiving the recognition and reward we feel we deserve for our service, that's no reason to throw in the towel. It's the easiest thing in the world to quit and give up. That's why there's little or no reward for it. On the other hand, when we remain diligent in our work for God, we show that we love Him and are serious about wanting to obey Him. And there are always rewards for obedience.

You and I weren't filled with the Spirit of God so that we could be quitters. We were given a new birth and a new nature so that we could serve God and others with the mindset that we are ultimately working for Him, and our reward will come from Him. (Ephesians 6:7-8) Scripture declares: "We're not quitters who lose out." (Hebrews 10:39 MSG) Ask yourself today, "What could it cost me if I quit and give up now?"

Lord, forgive me for the times that I left assignments from You unfinished. I don't want to be a sluggard who craves and ends up with nothing — I want to be a diligent worker who realizes the fulfillment of Your promises, and my dreams. Give me a spirit of diligence, and whenever I'm tempted to quit and give up, send me the encouragement I need to keep going. Thank You for the untold rewards I will reap when I determine to persist "to the very end"!

Promise-Power Point: Those things I hope for will be fully realized when I perform my God-given assignments with diligence.

Decisions and Dilemmas

"I am the Lord your God, who teaches you what is best for you, who directs you in the way you should go."
Isaiah 48:17 NIV

I heard from one of my readers who had been suffering with anxiety attacks for many months. She and her husband prayed earnestly for her deliverance and healing, but the attacks continued and even worsened. Finally, she sought medical attention and began therapy at her doctor's recommendation. As soon as she did, her husband made her feel guilty and condemned because he was convinced that her problem was entirely spiritual, and that by allowing a doctor to treat her condition, she was demonstrating a lack of faith. When she wrote me, she described her dilemma, and she asked me for my advice.

I told this dear lady that I couldn't tell her for certain, but that I suspected that it was the Lord who led her to seek medical attention when her attacks persisted and even worsened. I explained that even though it was very likely that there was a spiritual element to these attacks, she might still need to seek out some practical help for her condition – in this case, from a physician. I encouraged her to ask the Lord to give her clarity and confirmation in the matter, and to give Him the opportunity to do so by getting quiet before Him, and listening carefully for His voice. Sometimes, in cases like these, I will pray something like, "Lord, unless You clearly tell me otherwise, I am going to continue seeing this doctor for this condition. Above all, I want Your perfect will in this matter, so I am trusting You to lead me."

I pointed out to this dear woman that if she had been reading my devotionals on a regular basis, then she probably already knew that my husband, Joe, and I are not always in agreement with each other, and that I always put God's will and wisdom first. While it's nice when our spouses – or friends or loved ones – agree with us, there may be times when they are opposed to our decisions and choices, even when we are in agreement with God. We can ask the Lord to change their hearts, but if He doesn't, He will still expect us to faithfully follow His lead.

The Bible says: "I am the Lord your God, who teaches you what is best for you, who directs you in the way you should go." (Isaiah 48:17 NIV) This is a lofty claim, and only God Himself can make it. Even those people who love us most here on earth cannot see the future, or know with any certainty which is the best course for us to take when we have a decision to make. Only God can look ahead and see the consequences of every choice we make in our lifetime. And only He can love us with a perfect, selfless love. Even the most well-intentioned people have their own agendas when they offer us advice. So we need to be very careful who we listen to.

I have been a mother for 37 years, but even now, when my children ask me for advice, I rarely offer it without having at least prayed a quick and silent prayer, asking for the Lord's wisdom. And though my husband, Joe, and I have been together more than 40 years, it's not my habit to offer him counsel off the top of my head. Most of all, I encourage my loved ones to seek God's wisdom for themselves, so that they won't make decisions that they will regret later on.

Perhaps you are facing a dilemma of your own today. If so, one thing I can tell you with certainty is that God already knows what is best for you, and He will direct you, if you humbly seek His wisdom and will. Claim His promise of guidance today, and watch what He will do to lead you in the paths of His greatest blessings!

Lord, help me to always seek counsel from You before I go to other people. I believe that You have good plans for my life, and that You will help me to walk in them as I continually and consistently seek Your wisdom. Guard me from the doubt and deception that can cause me to stray from Your perfect pathway. Thank You that as I follow Your lead, I will learn firsthand what Your very best is for me every day in every way!

Promise-Power Point: God offers to teach me what is best for me in every situation, and as I choose His will and way, I will experience the abundant life that He has promised in His Word.

Get Out of the Way

"Do not be afraid. Stand firm and you will see the deliverance the Lord will bring you today. The Lord will fight for you; you need only to be still." Exodus 14:13,14 NIV

When I purchased a new printer for my home office recently, I asked my husband, Joe, to set it up for me. He started the task, but before he completed it, he left the room and went to do something else. As I sat there at my computer, I began thinking to myself, "He doesn't know how to hook up this new printer. Looks like I'll have to do without a printer for a while." Then, I got quiet in my spirit and began to pray that the Lord would intervene and help Joe to finish the job he started. Suddenly, I remembered some things that I had to do, and I got up and left my office. When I came back, my new printer was set up and working perfectly. When I went to thank my husband, he told me, "I was just waiting for you to get out of my way so that I could work!"

Later, the Lord showed me that He often feels the same way Joe does, when He wants to do a work in people's lives and circumstances, but we keep getting in His way. Let's face it, when we have a problem, or we long to see God working in our loved ones' lives, we can get pretty impatient, and we can start trying to make something happen on our own. This almost never works because the Lord usually prefers accomplishing His work when we are inclined to trust Him and wait on Him. Many years ago, I heard a very wise man say that the main reason why Christians lose so many battles is that they try to fight them themselves, instead of relying on God. I have learned the hard way just how true this is.

When Moses and the Israelites desperately needed to be rescued from the clutches of Pharaoh and the Egyptians, Moses spoke for God when he gave them this solemn warning: "Do not be afraid. Stand firm and you will see the deliverance the Lord will bring you today. The Lord will fight for you; you need only to be still." (Exodus 14:13,14 NIV) Take special note of the "be still" part of these verses. Being still in the midst of trouble and turmoil can be very difficult, but many times it is the very thing that will open the door to the miraculous. One reason why God honors our stillness is that it honors Him. It shows that we are trusting Him to do what only He can do. The Message Bible translation of Exodus 14:14 reads, "GOD will fight the battle for you. And you? You keep your mouths shut!" The Lord is prepared to work in your life and circumstances today. Are you prepared to be still, and to stay out of His way?

Lord, forgive me for the times that I failed to trust You and wait on You, and I only made a bigger mess of things. Help me to clearly discern when you want me to act, and when you want me to be still. When I am in the midst of trouble and turmoil, remind me that You might not do anything, unless I stay out of Your way. Thank You that as I cooperate with Your plans and purposes, I will see You change hearts and lives!

Promise-Power Point: When I demonstrate my trust in God through stillness and patience, I will set the stage for Him to move mightily on my behalf.

The Pain of Loss

"The Lord is close to those whose hearts are breaking." Psalm 34:18 TLB

Even for followers of Christ, life has a way of catching us off guard sometimes, and sending us into a tailspin – especially where suffering a loss is concerned. Whether it's the loss of a person, pet, or possession, the effects can be devastating. The good news is that as believers in Christ, we have heavenly resources in times of loss that can help us to heal and recover more quickly and completely than we ever could apart from God. Is it wrong to mourn the loss of a loved one? Absolutely not. Jesus Himself said, "Blessed are those who mourn, for they will be comforted." (Matthew 5:4 NIV) However, it is not the Lord's will for us to sink into a deep pit of depression when we are experiencing a profound sense of loss.

Perhaps you're familiar with the Scripture that says, "Do not grieve, for the joy of the Lord is your strength." (Nehemiah 8:10 NIV) But look at the Amplified translation of this verse, which provides us with even richer insights: "Be not grieved and depressed, for the joy of the Lord is your strength and stronghold." (Nehemiah 8:10 AMP) The kind of joy that believers have access to at all times through God's indwelling Spirit is a gift that infuses us with supernatural strength.

When Scripture says that this joy is a "stronghold," it is saying that it has the power to protect us against attack. The devil and his evil cohorts will not be able to drag us into a pit of despair when we continually walk in the joy of the Lord. How do we do that? By asking God for it, by clinging to His promises, and by making a quality decision to put our trust in Him. David prayed, "Bring joy to Your servant, Lord, for I put my trust in You." (Psalm 86:4 NIV)

I have discovered that praying God's promises in times of loss can bring great comfort and healing. Psalm 147:3 (AMP) says: "He heals the brokenhearted and binds up their wounds [curing their pains and their sorrows]." So when you pray, "Lord, heal my broken heart, bind up my wounds, and cure my pains and sorrows," you are praying the will of God, and you can be confident that the Lord will answer your prayers. (1 John 5:14-15)

When I am being assailed by grief and sorrow, I speak directly to them and tell them to GO in the name of Jesus, on the basis of God's Word in Isaiah 53:4 (NKJV), which says, "Surely [Jesus] has borne our griefs and carried our sorrows." You and I don't have to be a doormat for the devil. We have God-given authority from the King of Kings Himself to resist and rebuke the works of Satan, including the kind of grief and sorrow that come from the enemy. Jesus promised: "I have given you authority to trample on snakes and scorpions and to overcome all the power of the enemy; nothing will harm you." (Luke 10:19 NIV)

One of the best prayers that we can pray in times of loss is, "Lord, show me the good in all of this." We base this heartfelt prayer on God's own promise which says: "And we know that God causes all things to work together for good to those who love God, to those who are called according to His purpose." (Romans 8:28 NASB) Sometimes our circumstances are so devastating, and our pain so debilitating, that we cannot imagine anything positive coming from them. We need to ask for the Lord's perspective, and to pray that He will open our eyes to see the good that we will reap – if we will only respond to our loss in God-honoring ways.

If you are feeling the pain of loss today, please know that the Lord cares very much about your hurt and heartache, and He is there for you. Cling to Jesus' promise to His beloved ones in John 14:18 (KJV) – "I will not leave you comfortless; I will come to you."

Lord, when I suffer a loss of any kind, help me to turn to You first for help and healing. Show me the good in my situation, and reassure me that something positive will come from my pain. Teach me how to cling to Your life-giving promises, and how to stop the forces of darkness from causing me harm. Thank You that as I keep my trust in You and Your faithfulness, I will gain the victory that belongs to me in Christ!

Promise-Power Point: Because I am devoted to Christ, when I suffer a loss, I can call upon Him for help, comfort, and healing that no one else can offer, and I can expect Him to enable me to profit from my pain.

Dating: One Mom's Perspective

"Do not be conformed to this world (this age), [fashioned after and adapted to its external, superficial customs], but be transformed (changed) by the [entire] renewal of your mind [by its new ideals and its new attitude], so that you may prove [for yourselves] what is the good and acceptable and perfect will of God, even the thing which is good and acceptable and perfect [in His sight for you]." Romans 12:2 AMP

I often hear from people – both parents and children alike – who ask my opinion on dating, from a Christian perspective. I don't profess to be an expert by any means, but I do often share with them some of my own experiences as a parent. I tell them candidly that I did not allow my own sons to date until they were 18 years old. I came to this decision after much prayer, as well as the realization that I didn't want to automatically accept the world's view on dating. I recalled the fact that my father always regretted allowing my sisters and me to enter the "dating scene" when we were only 16 years of age, and as I looked back, I understood the basis for his regrets. All of us had experienced heartbreak and misery that we could have been spared if we had just waited for God's will and timing, where our relationships were concerned. When I finally made my decision about my sons, I began hearing disturbing warnings from other parents. Some said that I was robbing my children of healthy, valuable experiences that would benefit them later in life. Many said that my kids were "missing out". I must admit that there were times when I wavered, and wondered if I was being unreasonable or legalistic. It was especially difficult when I saw my sons struggling with feeling left out of groups of their peers that were all couples. But by the grace of God, we all got through it, and I believe to this day that I made the right decision in making them wait.

My older son, Joseph, has been married for almost 14 years to a wonderful young lady named Miriam, whom he met through his college Bible club. They met when they were both 18 years old, and they married after knowing each other for five years. Joseph and Miriam are deeply committed to each other, and I believe they have many happily married years ahead of them. My younger son, John, has been married for almost 11 years to Amy, a sweet young lady whom he met through his high school Bible club. They, too, married after being together for five years. Both Amy and Miriam are godly young women, and delightful additions to our family. And both are totally devoted to my sons. I don't bring all this up to boast or to tell you what you should do, but to give you an example of just how wrong some of the world's views on dating and child rearing can be. Yes, it's certainly true that my kids "missed out". They missed out on untold amounts of misery and heartbreak, as well as all the far-reaching, negative consequences of being involved with relationships that were out of God's will and timing for them. And while it was difficult for my family to take an unpopular stand, and to wait for what we believed was the Lord's timing, He rewarded us by blessing my sons with the perfect mates, without them having to go through a string of "imperfect" ones.

If you are a parent or a single person dealing with one side or another of this issue, let me encourage you today to give less attention to the world's ideas and standards for dating relationships, and more attention to God's. He alone knows what is best for you, and if you jump ahead of His perfect plan and timing in this area, you could very well delay or miss out on His best for you, or your children. Today, ask the Lord to give you some new attitudes, so that you will be able to see things His way from now on. And receive all the good things He has in store for you and yours!

Lord, forgive me for the times I have followed the ways of the world, instead of Your ways. Grant that I may be "constantly renewed in the spirit of my mind [having a fresh mental and spiritual attitude]" so that I may obey You in every area, and reap all the blessings You have for me and mine. (Ephesians 4:23 AMP) I pray that our relationships will be ALL that You want them to be, and ONLY what You want them to be!

Promise-Power Point: When I refuse to conform to the world's way of doing things, and instead adopt the ways of God, I will be able to know and carry out His divine purposes and plans for myself and my loved ones, which will lead to success and safety in every area of our lives.

Don't Fail to Ask

"I urge you to pray for absolutely everything, ranging from small to large. Include everything as you embrace this God-life, and you'll get God's everything." Mark 11:24 MSG

When my son, Joseph, and his wife, Miriam, visited us from California recently, he sent a text message to my cell phone saying that they were running late, and that they were probably going to miss their flight. That would mean that they would miss their connection in Chicago, too, and that they might not be able to arrive in Pennsylvania at all that evening. They were only coming for a weekend visit, so every moment counted on this trip.

Immediately, I turned to the Lord in prayer, and I asked Him to enable my son and his wife to make their flight out of California right on time. A short time later, I got another text from Joseph saying that they had made their flight, with time to spare. When I sent my son a text saying that I had been praying for them, and that I was giving God the glory, I got a text from him shortly afterwards saying that Miriam had told him, "I wonder how much wouldn't happen for us if your mom weren't praying for us!"

Miriam's words greatly encouraged my heart, because I do spend a lot of time in prayer for my loved ones each day. I know what a difference it can make, and how worth the time and effort it is. It wasn't always this way for me, though. Years ago, I spent very little time in prayer, and when I did pray, I didn't see the amazing answers to my prayers that I see now. It wasn't until I started studying the Scriptures diligently each day, and praying and standing on God's promises, that I began seeing the hand of God moving mightily on my behalf, and on behalf of my loved ones.

The Bible says: "You do not have because you do not ask God." (James 4:2 NIV) This verse literally changed my life, as well as my prayer life, when I began meditating on it, and applying it to big things and small. These days, I'm afraid NOT to pray about something, because I hate the idea of missing out on God's best in any situation. No concern is too small or trivial to take to the Lord in prayer. This may sound like an overstatement or exaggeration at first glance, but I assure you that it is not. If you agree with me on this point, but you seem to simply forget to pray about certain things, then ask the Holy Spirit to remind you to "pray about everything," as the Bible tells us to. (Philippians 4:6 NLT) Then rejoice and give God thanks, as you witness Him intervening mightily on your behalf!

Lord, I know that there have been times when it was Your desire for me to pray for someone, or about something, and I let You down. Teach me how to pray the prayers of Your heart in every situation and circumstance. Help me to get to know You better each day, so that I can learn to see things from Your perspective, and pray accordingly. Give me a greater understanding of the power behind my prayers because Your Spirit lives in me. Thank You for making me a world-changer for Christ through my prayer life!

Promise-Power Point: As I become sensitive and obedient to the Holy Spirit's promptings to pray according to God's will, I will experience answers to prayer that will change lives and circumstances for the glory of God, and the advancement of His Kingdom.

You Don't Have to Be Afraid

"Now may the Lord of peace Himself grant you His peace (the peace of His kingdom) at all times and in all ways [under all circumstances and conditions, whatever comes]." 2 Thessalonians 3:16 AMP

When I was outside tending to my ducks, Lily and Larry, one day, a hawk suddenly flew over our heads. The terror in my ducks' eyes was apparent, and they stiffened and became paralyzed with fear. I happened to be standing right next to them at the time, so I emphatically told them, "You have nothing to fear while I'm standing right beside you!" Even though I knew that hawks were a real threat to Lily and Larry, and that they could do them serious harm, I didn't understand their fearful behavior when it was obvious that their protector and provider was so very close by.

Suddenly, I heard the Lord's voice deep in my spirit say, "That's exactly how I feel when you forget that I am with you, and you become fearful and fretful." I instantly felt ashamed, and the Holy Spirit brought to my remembrance a verse from Isaiah 41:10 (AMP), which says: "Fear not [there is nothing to fear], for I am with you; do not look around you in terror and be dismayed, for I am your God. I will strengthen and harden you to difficulties, yes, I will help you; yes, I will hold you up and retain you with My [victorious] right hand of rightness and justice." The truth is that, for those of us who are abiding in Christ, "there is nothing to fear" when trouble comes. If I felt indignant and insulted when my ducks became afraid while I was standing right next to them, then imagine how the Lord feels when we become fearful every time we feel threatened in some way.

Jesus said: "Peace I leave with you; My [own] peace I now give and bequeath to you. Not as the world gives do I give to you. Do not let your hearts be troubled, neither let them be afraid. [Stop allowing yourselves to be agitated and disturbed; and do not permit yourselves to be fearful and intimidated and cowardly and unsettled.]" (John 14:27 AMP) You and I have the privilege of claiming the peace of Christ in the midst of our trials, and we don't have to allow ourselves to be intimidated by circumstances, other people, or the devil himself. The next time trouble comes knocking on your door, remember that you have a choice. Take your stand in faith and declare with confidence – "I choose peace, in Jesus' name!"

Lord, please forgive me for the times that I allowed myself to become intimidated, fearful, and unsettled when I felt threatened in any way. Give me a trusting heart that stays calm and confident in the midst of trouble and turmoil. Remind me that You are the Prince of Peace, and that because Your Spirit dwells in me, I can draw on Your peace at all times. Help me to plant Your promises in my heart in ways that will strengthen my faith. Today, I refuse and resist all fear and dread, and I choose to walk in Your supernatural peace!

Promise-Power Point: *Christ offers me divine protection as I walk in obedience to Him, so I no longer have to succumb to the fear and intimidation that people, circumstances, or the devil threaten me with.*

Excuses or Freedom?

"But every person is tempted when he is drawn away, enticed and baited by his own evil desire (lust, passions)." James 1:14 AMP

In my daily quiet time with the Lord recently, I was talking to Him about certain areas of my life where I wasn't enjoying the freedom in Christ that I knew I should have. I asked Him where I was "missing it," and He led me to a verse in the book of James that really opened my eyes. "But every person is tempted when he is drawn away, enticed and baited by his own evil desire (lust, passions)." (James 1:14 AMP) Immediately, I recognized my self-defeating habit of blaming external forces for my failures, and I allowed the Holy Spirit to minister truth to me that set my feet on the path of victory.

To live the lives of freedom that Jesus bought for us on Calvary, we must acknowledge that it's our own evil desires that bait us and draw us away from the will of God. For example: I recently decided that I was going to be more serious about eating healthy. Just making the decision was tough enough, but it got even tougher when my husband, Joe, and I went out to eat on our weekly date night. When I placed my order, I managed to make all good, healthy choices. But my husband didn't. And when the food came to the table, I caved in and ate some of the rich and fattening foods, as well as the healthy ones. Later, as I complained to the Lord about it, and gave my husband most of the blame for my failure, He reminded me of the verse above in James that points to my own ungodly desires as being the true culprit. That's when I decided that I was no longer going to blame my husband, the devil, or anyone else for my failures. I told myself – "No more excuses!" – because I began to realize that if I continued to excuse my behavior for any reason, I would never be free.

With the realization that I had no one to blame but myself, I became filled with a holy determination to gain the victory. Sometimes, this kind of Spirit-inspired determination comes automatically when we need to make some changes in our lives, and other times we have to earnestly and continually pray for it. A good definition of "determination" is: "The act of deciding definitely and firmly; a firm or fixed intention to achieve a desired end." God wants to help us succeed, but He's not going to do it all for us. We have to be serious enough about walking in victory and freedom to make a firm decision to do whatever it is we have to do to be free. Once we determine to do our part, the Lord will give us a custom-made plan for our victory. Then we have to follow this divine plan by being sensitive and obedient to the promptings of the Holy Spirit on a moment-by-moment basis. The apostle Paul wrote: "But I say, walk and live [habitually] in the [Holy] Spirit [responsive to and controlled and guided by the Spirit];

then you will certainly not gratify the cravings and desires of the flesh (of human nature without God)." (Galatians 5:16 AMP) The same power that raised Christ from the dead is available to you and me every moment of every day, through the Spirit of God who dwells in us. (Ephesians 1:19-20) Yielding to the directing and empowering ministry of the Holy Spirit enables us to conquer our sinful desires. So, each time I sense God's Spirit saying, "Don't eat that" or "Don't do that," I will gain a greater measure of freedom by following His lead.

It's absolutely essential that we constantly remind ourselves of God's life-changing truths. Look at these powerful verses from the book of Romans penned by Paul: "We know that our old sinful selves were crucified with Christ so that sin might lose its power in our lives. We are no longer slaves to sin. For when we died with Christ we were set free from the power of sin." (Romans 6:6-7 NLT) Meditating on Scriptures like these will help us to say "no" to sin when the devil or our own carnal minds try to tell us that we are not equipped to succeed. Paul goes on to say: "So you also should consider yourselves to be dead to the power of sin and alive to God through Christ Jesus." (Romans 6:11 NLT) If we don't "consider" ourselves to be dead to sin, it will control our lives, even though we possess the power to overcome it. Paul reassures us that victory is within our reach, when he says: "But now you are free from the power of sin and have become slaves of God. Now you do those things that lead to holiness and result in eternal life." (Romans 6:22 NLT) If you long for a greater measure of victory and freedom as a follower of Christ, ask yourself today – "How badly do I want to be free?"

Lord, I confess the times that I allowed sin to rule over me, instead of following the leading of the Holy Spirit. Help me to do whatever it is I need to do to become all that You created me to be. Thank You that Your Spirit and Your Word will make me victorious for Your glory!

Promise-Power Point: Through Christ, I have the potential and the power to break free from every evil addiction and bondage, and as I yield to His Spirit's leading, I will gain the freedom He purchased for me on the Cross.

The Rewards of Endurance

"May the Lord bring you into an ever deeper understanding of the love of God and the endurance that comes from Christ." (2 Thessalonians 3:5 NLT)

When my husband, Joe, had to undergo open heart surgery for a failing valve, I learned the meaning and value of the kind of endurance that the Bible teaches. In addition to my own daily chores and responsibilities, I had to shoulder many of those that my husband regularly performed, and I felt myself being stretched physically and emotionally. As I turned to the Lord for help, He began teaching me how to practice endurance, as I sought Him daily in focused prayer and Scripture study.

The dictionary defines "endurance" as: "The ability or strength to continue or last – especially despite fatigue, stress, or other adverse conditions." As followers of Christ, you and I don't have to depend on our own "ability or strength" in stressful times; we can rely on His Spirit within us to empower and enable us to do whatever it is we need to do – and to do it all with a good attitude.

One of the dangers of failing to exercise endurance during stressful times is reaping the penalty of a wrong response. When hardships and heartaches come, we can be tempted to become angry, bitter, and resentful.

We can start pointing fingers and blaming others for our troubles. And we can forfeit the solutions, promotions, and rewards that the Lord had in store for us, because of His promise to work all things together for our good. (Romans 8:28) The apostle Paul wrote: "We try to live in such a way that no one will be hindered from finding the Lord by the way we act, and so no one can find fault with our ministry. In everything we do we try to show that we are true ministers of God. We patiently endure troubles and hardships and calamities of every kind." (2 Corinthians 6:3-4 NLT) The Lord wants to use our trials to reveal Himself to others by enabling us to display His peace and patience through them all. When people see that God is the source of our strength, they will be drawn to Him. And they will be more receptive when we try to tell them about Him.

The apostle Paul was a perfect example of someone who responded wisely to troubles and trials. It's no wonder, then, that God used him mightily, and that his testimony is still changing lives today. Paul wrote: "We think you ought to know, dear brothers and sisters, about the trouble we went through in the province of Asia. We were crushed and overwhelmed beyond our ability to endure, and we thought we would never live through it. In fact, we expected to die. But as a result, we stopped relying on ourselves and learned to rely only on God, who raises the dead." (2 Corinthians 1:8-9

NLT) You and I can stop relying on ourselves and learn to rely on God, just as Paul did. When we do, we will experience the resurrection power that lifts us above our circumstances, and enables us to walk in the victory that belongs to us in Christ.

The Bible reveals that we often need endurance in order to perform the will of God, and receive the fulfillment of His promises. "Do not throw away this confident trust in the Lord. Remember the great reward it brings you! Patient endurance is what you need now, so that you will continue to do God's will. Then you will receive all that He has promised." (Hebrews 10:35-36 NLT) Notice the word "continue". Many times, we begin following God's lead, and then we quit and give up before we reach the finish line. That's not the Lord's best for us. He wants us to stick with Him and His plans for us, until we attain and gain all of the good things He has for us. Right now, ask yourself what you stand to lose if you fail to practice endurance in the midst of your present difficulties. My prayer for you today is "that you'll have the strength to stick it out over the long haul — not the grim strength of gritting your teeth but the glory-strength God gives. It is strength that endures the unendurable and spills over into joy, thanking the Father who makes us strong enough to take part in everything bright and beautiful that He has for us"! (Colossians 1:11-12 MSG)

Lord, on the basis of Your Word, I pray that You would strengthen me with all of Your glorious power, so that I will have all the endurance I need to do Your will in every situation and circumstance. (Colossians 1:11 NLT) Give me a heart like Yours so that I can treat people with Christlike compassion when I am in the midst of stressful times. Thank You that as I choose Your way and Your will, I will reap every blessing and reward that You have in store for me!

Promise-Power Point: I don't have to rely on my own strength and ability in difficult times, but I can draw on the same power that raised Christ from the dead because the Spirit of the living God dwells in me.

A God of Deliverances

"He has delivered us from such a deadly peril, and He will deliver us again. On Him we have set our hope that He will continue to deliver us." 2 Corinthians 1:10 NIV

When my husband, Joe, and I were going through a very difficult and scary time financially, the Lord brought the verse above to my remembrance. I had claimed this promise many times, and this particular time, I was feeling a bit hesitant to do so. It seemed as though I was always asking the Lord to deliver my family and me in one regard or another. And I was getting weary of hearing myself claim this promise over and over again.

Then the Lord showed me that He inspired Paul to write this passage in the Bible to encourage us, not to convict us. He wanted us to know that His mercy, goodness, and desire to help us never wear out. Notice that God is NOT saying, "Well, I see that you're in trouble yet again. Don't think that I'm going to bail you out every time you have a problem. I'm through rescuing you!" No. When we have put our faith in Christ as our Savior, and have been adopted into God's family, we have the privilege of asking Almighty God to help us in our time of need — no matter how many times a need arises.

Yes, there are times when the Lord must allow us to suffer the natural consequences of our poor choices and decisions. But even then, He will not turn away from us when we turn to Him for help. The Lord longs for us to humble ourselves before Him, to repent for anything we might have done to invite our troubles, and to ask Him to forgive us and send us the kind of help that only He can give.

The Bible says, "God is to us a God of deliverances." (Psalm 68:20 NASB) It is our God's very nature to want to deliver His people when they are in trouble. Paul discovered this truth and declared, "He *has* delivered us...and He *will* deliver us *again*. On Him we have set our hope that He will *continue* to deliver us."

If you are in trouble today, and you have rightly placed your hope in the Lord for your deliverance, you have His assurance that His help is on the way!

Lord, Your Word makes it clear that You delight in delivering Your people. Teach me how to live for You, and how to rely on You for all my needs. When I am in trouble, show me how to position myself to receive the rescue You have in store for me. Help me to learn from my mistakes, but when I do repeat them, don't let me stubbornly refuse or neglect Your help. Today, I choose to look to You for rescue and relief!

Promise-Power Point: As I decide to see my God as the Deliverer that He is, and to believe in His earnest desire to deliver me in every situation, I will witness His awesome power on my behalf.

Fasting for Freedom

"And [Jesus] replied to them, 'This kind cannot be driven out by anything but prayer and fasting.'" Mark 9:29 AMP

Over the years, when I have struggled with certain sins, even though I have done my best to overcome them, the Lord has often led me to use a type of fasting to gain the victory. I'm not talking about a fast from food, necessarily, but a fast from sinful behavior. I am continually amazed by how powerful and effective this principle can be in the fight against habitual sins. My most recent battle has been with a persistent craving for sweets. It became so serious a problem that it literally threatened my health and well-being. As I cried out to the Lord for deliverance, He reminded me of Jesus' words in Mark 9:29 (AMP): "This kind cannot be driven out by anything but prayer and fasting." I knew then that my battle was definitely spiritual, and that it would take spiritual weapons to gain the victory — weapons like prayer and fasting. I made the decision to fast from sweets until I no longer craved them. It was extremely difficult for me at first, but it became easier as I persevered. And the blessed sense of freedom that I'm reaping now has made the painful process more than worth it.

Jesus taught that we should deal as drastically with sin as necessary when He said: "If your right eye causes you to sin, gouge it out and throw it away. It is better for you to lose one part of your body than for your whole body to be thrown into hell. And if your right hand causes you to sin, cut it off and throw it away. It is better for you to lose one part of your body than for your whole body to go into hell." (Matthew 5:29-30 NIV) Using this principle, we can fast from those things that LEAD us into sin. For instance, if we have a problem with alcohol, we can fast from those places and things that tempt us to overindulge. If we are wrestling with pornography or improper relationships online, we can fast from using the internet. If overspending is a problem for us, we can fast going to the mall. I've even known people who quit smoking cigarettes after hearing me teach on this subject in the past. Something supernatural happens when we declare a fast before the Lord. We do what we can do, and God does what we cannot do. As Jesus said, "What is impossible for people is possible with God." (Luke 18:27 NLT)

One word of caution: It might be wise for you to keep your fasting largely to yourself. (Matthew 6:17-18) Sometimes, telling others will tempt them to sabotage your efforts, either intentionally or unintentionally. Your change of behavior may cause them to feel threatened, especially if they are weighed down by the same sin you are struggling with. They may even view your rejection of the sinful behavior as rejection of them. Don't be surprised if the Lord asks you to end relationships that are hindering you from moving forward with Him and His plans for you.

When you are in the midst of a difficult fast, remind God that you are depending upon Him for help, and keep your eye on the rewards ahead. Jesus clearly stated that we would reap rewards for our fasting. (Matthew 6:17-18) Many times, our reward will be a greater degree of freedom. Don't be afraid to start out small. God can multiply your efforts and cause them to add up to tremendous progress. My prayer for you today is that you will call upon the Lord, and ask Him how using these powerful spiritual principles can help you gain true victory and freedom in Christ!

Lord, thank You for the powerful spiritual practice of fasting. Show me how You would like me to apply it to my life and my behaviors today. I don't want anything to hinder me from fulfilling my God-given purpose and potential. I want to walk in the total freedom that Christ bought for me on the Cross with His own precious blood. Today, I choose to lay hold of the blessed rewards that You have promised me when I fast Your way!

Promise-Power Point: *God has given me powerful tools in prayer and fasting, and as I follow His lead in applying them to my ungodly habits, I will experience the freedom, healing, and well-being that are my inheritance in Christ.*

Submit to God's Good Plans

"Submit yourselves, then, to God. Resist the devil, and he will flee from you." James 4:7 NIV

The scriptural promise above assures us that no matter what comes against us, if we will submit ourselves to the Lord, and resist the devil's tactics, he will have to flee from us. A man who wrote me recently gave me a perfect example of what happens when we submit to the devil's plans and purposes for us, instead of God's.

When it was discovered that this man's wife had terminal cancer, he earnestly prayed that God would heal her. He pleaded with the Lord that if it was not His will to restore her to health, that He would at least give this husband the cancer instead. A day or two before the wife's surgery, her symptoms disappeared. When the doctors operated on her, they found nothing – no cancer, and no disease. Several months later, this man was diagnosed with cancer himself. It was in the early stages and very treatable, but this man learned a valuable lesson that he is sharing with everyone today – be careful what you pray or wish for.

This man's testimony reminded me of one that I heard from my grandmother when I was a little girl. After the birth of her first child, she developed an illness that put her life at risk. Distraught, my grandfather told my ailing grandmother that he wished he could take her illness upon himself. Not long afterwards, my grandfather contracted a serious illness and died before the birth of their second child, my father. My grandmother related these events to me and my sisters while we were growing up in order to warn us about asking and praying for the wrong things.

When someone we care about deeply is ill or suffering in some way, it can be tempting for us to pray or wish that we could take their affliction upon ourselves. But when we do this, we are not submitting ourselves to God, as the verse above instructs us to, but we are actually submitting ourselves to the devil. Jesus said that Satan "comes only in order to steal and kill and destroy," but that He came so that we could "have and enjoy life". (John 10:10 AMP) In other words, we are to pray for and expect good things from God, and we are to resist praying for and expecting things that are likely to have the devil at their source – including sickness, calamity, poverty, and defeat.

The Bible says that we are created in the image of God Himself. (Genesis 1:26) And just as His words have power, ours do, too. With our words, including our prayers, we can open and close doors in the spiritual realm. When we ask and pray for the things that God calls good in His Word, then we open the door to His blessings and perfect plans for our lives. On the other hand, when we ask and pray for the things that the Bible says are evil, we open the door to Satan's evil plans and purposes for us. Ask yourself today, "Am I praying and believing for good things for myself and others?"

Lord, give me a keen awareness of just how powerful my words and my wishes can be. Help me to resist the devil and his evil devices every time by submitting myself to You and Your plans for me. Today, I choose to align my will and my ways with Yours, so that the forces of darkness have no power over me!

Promise-Power Point: When I submit myself to God – and resist the devil – in my thoughts, my words, and my actions, the evil one has no choice but to flee from me.

The Best Place for Burdens

"Casting the whole of your care [all your anxieties, all your worries, all your concerns, once and for all] on Him, for He cares for you affectionately and cares about you watchfully." 1 Peter 5:7 AMP

When I was a young wife and mother years ago, I suffered from bouts of anxiety and depression. As I look back, I am so grateful that I sought counseling, because I learned a lot during those therapy sessions. As I poured my heart out to my counselor, who was a devout Christian, she told me, "You can't bleed for everyone, Joanne." This woman wisely discerned that whenever I saw someone hurting – especially my loved ones – I would become burdened with their problems to the point of hurting myself. It was a self-destructive pattern that was harming me physically, mentally, and emotionally.

While the counseling that I had did help me in many ways, I never received the deliverance I so desperately needed until I began walking closely with the Lord years later, and began delving into the healing words of Scripture. I discovered King David's wise advice in Psalm 55: "Give your burdens to the Lord. He will carry them. He will not permit the godly to slip or fall." (Psalm 55:22 TLB) And I rejoiced. The truth that God didn't want me carrying anyone's burdens – including my own – set me free. And once I secured my freedom, the Lord was able to use me to minister to many hurting people on a regular basis, without hurting myself.

The apostle Peter reiterates David's admonition when he writes: "Give all your worries and cares to God, for He cares about you." (1 Peter 5:7 NLT) It's because the Lord cares so deeply for us that He doesn't want us being burdened with cares that have the potential to do us harm.

I sometimes think of that dear counselor who helped me those many years ago, and I have to smile. I wonder what she would say if she knew that I now minister to countless hurting people on a regular basis, without hurting myself. How do I do it? I carry their burdens to the Lord in prayer, instead of carrying their burdens myself. And with God's help, you can do the same.

Lord, forgive me for the times I have tried to fulfill Your role by taking on people's problems that You never meant me to. Give me the discernment and self-control I need to refuse to be burdened in ways that would harm me. Remind me often that You are the great Burden-Bearer (Psalm 68:19), and that it is never Your will for me to be crushed under the weight of my problems, or anyone else's. Today, I choose to cast ALL of my anxieties, burdens, and cares upon You, because You care for me!

Promise-Power Point: As I make a habit of carrying my burdens — and the burdens of others — to God in prayer, I will experience the peace, relief, and freedom that are my inheritance in Christ.

Opportunities and Adversaries

"Fear not; for those with us are more than those with them." 2 Kings 6:16 AMP

It's been said that there are 365 commands to "Fear not!" in the Bible. One reason for this is that when we decide to live for God, and to follow His call on our life, we will encounter spiritual resistance from the forces of darkness. My husband, Joe, and I experienced this recently when we were working together on a ministry project that we felt led by God to do. At one point, we encountered so many obstacles and hindrances, that our frustration and discouragement began to get the best of us. And we were tempted to quit. "Maybe this project isn't the Lord's will after all," was one conclusion that we began considering. As I sought God for clarification and confirmation, He led me to the promise above.

These are the words of the great prophet Elisha to his fearful servant when they were surrounded by enemy forces. While Elisha had the ability to see into the spirit realm, his servant could only see what was happening in the natural realm. So Elisha prayed, "Open his eyes, Lord, so that he may see." Suddenly, the servant "looked and saw the hills full of horses and chariots of fire all around Elisha." (2 Kings 6:17 NIV) As I contemplated these things, I knew in my heart that God was telling me to persevere, because we were doing His work, and He would fight our battles for us.

From then on, I declared over and over, "I will not fear, because those who are with us are more than those who are with them!" As my fears subsided, I gained new strength and resolve to finish the work, and I was able to encourage my husband, just as Elisha had encouraged his servant.

The apostle Paul wrote: "A wide door of opportunity for effectual [service] has opened to me [there, a great and promising one], and [there are] many adversaries." (1 Corinthians 16:9 AMP) One reason why Paul made such a powerful and lasting impact upon this world was that God gave him many "great and promising" opportunities for service. But along with them, came great opposition from earthly and spiritual forces. When you and I commit our lives to the Lord, and ask Him to put us to work in His kingdom, He will do exactly that. But we have to remember that like Paul, we will often encounter resistance from hostile forces. If we will keep our eyes on God, and seek His plan for our victory and success, we will have all the power and resources of Heaven on our side!

Lord, thank You for the gifts and skills You've given me. Today, I commit them to You, and I ask that You use them for Your glory. Put me to work in Your Kingdom. Give me opportunities for service that will make a real difference in this world. When I encounter resistance of any kind, lead me to seek You for guidance and strength. Thank You that no matter what or who comes against me, I will gain the victory as I follow Your winning battle plan!

Promise-Power Point: *Though I face many adversaries when God opens doors of opportunity for me, I will not be defeated if I will trust Him to supply everything I need to succeed.*

Holding On to Our Healing

"Jesus said to him, 'Receive your sight; your faith has healed you.' Immediately he received his sight and followed Jesus, praising God. When all the people saw it, they also praised God." Luke 18:42-43 NIV

There are times when we are earnestly praying for healing of some kind, and our prayers seem to go unanswered. When this happened to me recently, and I asked the Lord where I was missing it, He led me to the account of Jesus healing a blind man in Luke 18:42-43 (NIV). As I began meditating on these verses, the word "receive" seemed to jump off the page. Jesus told the man, "Receive your sight; your faith has healed you." It was as if He were saying, "Take your healing by faith!" We see in the very next verse that the blind man did exactly that when the Scripture says, "Immediately he received his sight." In other words, that man laid hold of his healing right away. He didn't hesitate or doubt. He took Jesus at His word, and with His faith, He grabbed a hold of the healing that was being held out to him. You and I can do the same thing. We can pray for healing and then declare, "I receive my healing, in Jesus' name!" Once we have crossed that "faith line," we can proclaim, "I have my healing!" every time we begin to waver or doubt. And the Lord will back up our words of faith.

But how can we cooperate with God to keep our healing once we receive it? Let's look at this formerly blind man's response to his healing. The Scripture says that he "followed Jesus". He didn't just receive his healing and then wander off, never to be seen again. No, he made the decision to follow the Savior. He became a Christ-follower. Many people who pray for, and receive, their healing eventually lose it unnecessarily. They go back to their old ways. They don't spend regular time in God's presence, or in His Word. Their lives, and their lifestyles, don't change in any real way, and they become easy targets for the devil and his evil cohorts, whose objective is only to "steal and kill and destroy," as Jesus said. (John 10:10)

The Lord has better plans for you and me. When we receive our healing from God, we can seek Him to find out exactly what He wants us to do to keep our healing. He may require us to change some habits which He knows are harming our health. And, very likely, He will expect us to get to know Him and His Word better, so we can experience all the good plans He has in store for us. Whatever it is the Lord is asking us to do, if we will follow His lead, we will continue to enjoy the renewed health that He has blessed us with.

Luke 18:43 also reveals that when the blind man received his healing, he began "praising God". This is a powerful principle for Christ-followers to learn. When the Lord heals us, even if He uses doctors or medicines in the process, we must recognize that God is still the Healer, and all of our thanks and praise belong to Him. Isaiah 42:8 (NLT) says: "I am the Lord; that is My name! I will not give My glory to anyone else, nor share My praise..." Failing to give God the glory due Him can jeopardize our healing, as well as our other blessings. In the Bible account of Jesus healing the ten lepers, we find out that only one of the healed men came back to give the Lord thanks and praise. He didn't just thank the Savior once, but according to Scripture, he thanked Him "over and over". (Luke 17:16 AMP) My guess is that this wise man never lost his healing, but I have to wonder about the other ungrateful nine.

The last part of Luke 18:43 reveals that the blind man's healing – and his demonstration of gratitude to God – caused others to give the Lord praise. One reason why God delights in healing us is that it brings Him glory, and draws others to Him. What can you do to cooperate with the Lord for your healing today?

Lord, whenever I need healing in my mind, heart, or body, remind me to turn to You first. Teach me, not only how to pray for my healing, but how to receive my healing from You. Show me what I need to do to keep my healing, and help me to cooperate with You wholeheartedly to that end. Thank You that as I give You all the thanks and the praise, lives will be changed for Your glory!

Promise-Power Point: The Lord doesn't only want me to RECEIVE my healing from Him, but He also wants me to KEEP my healing, and He will show me how to do that if I will seek His wisdom, and give Him the devotion and praise that He deserves.

Free from Condemnation

"So now there is no condemnation for those who belong to Christ Jesus." Romans 8:1 NLT

One thing I have discovered since I've been in a position to minister to large numbers of believers is that many of them continually struggle with feelings of guilt and condemnation. If you are one of these people, let me first say that I sympathize with you, because I know how you feel. For most of my years as a believer, I had the same struggles. But I'm happy to say that I am gaining more and more victory in this area all the time, and I am determined to persevere until I experience the kind of freedom Christ died for me to have. You can do the same.

First, accept responsibility for your sin. Whenever we do wrong, there's a part of us — the carnal, fleshly part — that wants to deny or ignore our wrongdoing. If we give in to that temptation, we will become burdened with feelings of condemnation. Why? Because followers of Christ have the Holy Spirit dwelling on the inside of them, and His job is to convict us when we sin against God. This conviction creates an inner tension that simply will not go away until we admit our wrongdoing and ask for forgiveness. The Bible says: "If we claim to be without sin, we deceive ourselves and the truth is not in us... If we claim we have not sinned, we make [God] out to be a liar and His word has no place in our lives." (1 John 1:8,10 NIV) Unconfessed sin is rooted in deception. It keeps us in bondage. And it has the potential to hinder our prayers and our fellowship with God. As Scripture says: "If I had cherished sin in my heart, the Lord would not have listened; but God has surely listened and heard my voice in prayer." (Psalm 66:18-19 NIV)

Confession and repentance are essential to living free from condemnation. As believers, it's imperative that we make a regular practice of confronting, confessing, and turning away from our wrongdoing. The Bible says: "If we confess our sins to Him, He can be depended on to forgive us and to cleanse us from every wrong. And it is perfectly proper for God to do this for us because Christ died to wash away our sins." (1 John 1:9 TLB) The truth is that there is great power in repentance. When we freely admit our sins and ask the Lord to help us overcome them, we invite the purifying power of God to bear on our tendencies for wrongdoing. That's one of the reasons why, when we sin, Satan and his dark forces will do everything they can to keep us from turning to the Lord in heartfelt repentance. They will tell us, "You've gone too far now. There's no hope for you. Don't think God is going to forgive you this time." If we refuse to buy into these lies, we will experience the comfort and cleansing that the Lord promises His repentant children.

Receiving God's forgiveness is an important part of experiencing freedom from condemnation. If you are one of the many believers who finds receiving God's forgiveness too difficult, then the next time you confess your sin, say out loud, "I receive Your forgiveness, Lord, and I thank You for it in Jesus' name." Believe that God is eager to extend mercy toward you, just as His Word promises. "Let us then fearlessly and confidently and boldly draw near to the throne of grace (the throne of God's unmerited favor to us sinners), that we may receive mercy [for our failures] and find grace to help in good time for every need [appropriate help and well-timed help, coming just when we need it.]." (Hebrews 4:16 AMP) And the Lord doesn't stop at extending mercy toward us, but He goes even further by giving us the grace we need to gain the victory.

Jesus said: "I tell you the truth, those who listen to My message and believe in God who sent Me have eternal life. They will never be condemned for their sins, but they have already passed from death into life." (John 5:24 NLT) If you have trusted Christ as your Savior, and have made Him the Lord of your life, you don't have to live under condemnation. Believe it – and receive your deliverance today!

Lord, help me to be ever mindful that when I sin, I need to confess my sin to You, repent for my wrongdoing, and receive Your forgiveness and cleansing. Remind me often that because of Christ's sacrifice, I am a "new creation," and I am no longer a slave to sin. (2 Corinthians 5:17; Romans 6:6-7) Thank You that as I trust in Your promises and depend on Your Spirit, I will live the overcoming life that You bought for me on Calvary! (1 John 5:4)

Promise-Power Point: **I do not have to live under guilt and condemnation when I freely confess my sins, and look to God for the help I need to live a godly life.**

A Lifetime Savior

"He will feed His flock like a shepherd. He will carry the lambs in His arms, holding them close to His heart. He will gently lead the mother sheep with their young."
Isaiah 40:11 NLT

Some of the most comforting promises in all of Scripture can be found in Isaiah 40:11. Here, the prophet Isaiah paints a portrait of the coming Messiah hundreds of years before He is born in a manger in Bethlehem. He writes: "He will feed His flock like a shepherd. He will carry the lambs in His arms, holding them close to His heart. He will gently lead the mother sheep with their young." (Isaiah 40:11 NLT) If we take a close look at this blessing-enriched verse, we can gain a greater understanding of all that it promises to the Lord's devoted ones.

"He will feed His flock like a shepherd," speaks of provision for the faithful. Jesus confirms this when He tells His followers — who He senses are anxious about having their needs met — "Your heavenly Father already knows perfectly well the things you need, and He will give them to you if you give Him first place in your life and live as He wants you to." (Matthew 6:32-33 TLB) My family and I are living proof of the truth of this promise, and so are countless other believers throughout the ages. When we order our priorities in line with God's, He takes on the responsibility of providing for us, and He makes certain that we have everything we need to live the abundant life He has called us to.

I especially love how Isaiah says that our Good Shepherd "will carry the lambs in His arms." When we are feeling weak and weary, we can ask the Lord to lift us up and carry us to safety and blessing. Now that I am older, I cherish the Lord's words that promise, "I will be your God throughout your lifetime – until your hair is white with age. I made you, and I will care for you. I will carry you along and save you." (Isaiah 46:4 NLT) Notice that the Lord does not say, "I will drag you along…" No, it is His desire and delight to carry us to safety in our time of need, especially when we ask Him to.

Next, Isaiah writes that the Messiah holds us close to His heart. The Lord doesn't keep His devoted ones at a distance; He draws us close to Him, and He holds us firmly and lovingly in good times and bad. Pondering this word picture, I can't help thinking of David the shepherd-king's words in Psalm 27: "Even if my father and mother abandon me, the Lord will hold me close." (Psalm 27:10 NLT) Here is a precious promise for those who have ever felt betrayed or neglected by a parent. I know people who were told by their parents, "You were a mistake. I never wanted you." If you are one of these people, let me tell you with all certainty that God wanted you! And He has glorious plans for your life that you will experience if you follow Him.

"He will gently lead the mother sheep with their young," means that the Lord will offer us His guidance, as long as we are letting Him take the lead. This promise gave me great comfort when my children were younger, and I desperately needed God's wisdom. When I didn't know what to do as a parent, God knew, and He shared His knowledge with me as I humbly sought His direction. In David's famous 23rd Psalm, where He speaks of the Lord as our Shepherd, he writes: "Even when walking through the dark valley of death I will not be afraid, for You are close beside me, guarding, guiding all the way." (Psalm 23: 4 TLB) We can trust that when the Lord leads us, He is always guiding us away from danger and destruction, and into the blessings, opportunities, and rewards that He has for us. Are you ready and willing to yield to the Good Shepherd's leadership today?

Lord, teach me to live for You so that I can reap the rewards of Your promised provision. When I am feeling worn out and weary, lift me up and carry me to Your place of refreshment and healing. Let me feel You holding me close to Your heart, especially when hardship or heartache come my way. Guide me continually with Your divine wisdom, and make me receptive to Your leadership. Today, I choose to love You, follow You, and worship You with all my heart!

Promise-Power Point: I am not alone in this world, but I have a Savior who will provide for me, carry me, and guide me throughout my lifetime, as I live my life for Him.

Benefits and Blessings from God

"The merciful, kind, and generous man benefits himself [for his deeds return to bless him], but he who is cruel and callous [to the wants of others] brings on himself retribution." Proverbs 11:17 AMP

This past winter brought more ice and snow to the East Coast than my husband, Joe, and I had ever seen in our 60+ years. The worst part was that as soon as one storm was over, another one was on its way. Joe would be out there morning and night using his snow blower on our property, and then using it to help neighbors who had no snow blower of their own. It was hard work, especially for someone like Joe who had suffered a heart attack one year, and then undergone open-heart surgery another. Nevertheless, Joe wasn't the type to turn his back on a neighbor in need, so storm after storm, he labored to clear away the snow and ice for us, and for others.

All those storms were very hard on our old snow blower, and one day, our old machine refused to start. So Joe began the hard task of shoveling our long driveway and walkways by hand. I was busy inside our house, and when it dawned on me that I hadn't heard the familiar sound of our snow blower, I took a peek outside one of our front windows. What I saw made tears spring to my eyes. Two of our neighbors who didn't have snow blowers were busy shoveling our driveway, while Joe stood by trying to catch his breath. One of these neighbors was an elderly gentleman who never shoveled his own property, but always hired someone younger and more able to do it. The other neighbor was the man who hired himself out to our elderly neighbor, to earn some extra money to pay his bills. Both were neighbors that Joe had helped out many times when storms had covered their property with ice and snow.

As I watched this scene of neighborly love, I thought about Solomon's words in the Book of Proverbs: "The merciful, kind, and generous man benefits himself [for his deeds return to bless him]." (Proverbs 11:17 AMP) Another proverb of the wise king in this chapter says: "A generous man will prosper; he who refreshes others will himself be refreshed." (Proverbs 11:25 NIV) You see, our God is a generous God, and He calls His people to follow His example. He does this, not just so we can be a blessing to others, but so we will benefit ourselves. The apostle Paul put it this way: "[Remember] this: he who sows sparingly and grudgingly will also reap sparingly and grudgingly, and he who sows generously [that blessings may come to someone] will also reap generously and with blessings." (2 Corinthians 9:6 AMP) Even if we don't receive rewards for our acts of generosity from other people, God will reward us Himself. I know this from experience because when I have labored long and hard without any apparent reward for my efforts, the Lord has led me to claim His promise in Isaiah 49:4 (NIV): "But I said, 'I have labored in vain; I have spent my strength for nothing at all. Yet what is due me is in the Lord's hand, and my reward is with my God.'" And I have witnessed God sending me blessings that I never could have imagined, or even asked for. The Bible says, "Kindness makes a man (or woman) attractive." (Proverbs 19:22 TLB) Are you ready to get better looking God's way?

Lord, forgive me for the times that You've sent opportunities my way to be a blessing to others, and I didn't make the most of them. Give me a generous and compassionate heart like Yours, so that I will be eager to reach out to others using the strength and the skills You've blessed me with. Help me to have pure motives that are pleasing to You when I lend someone a hand. Thank You that when my efforts are unappreciated and overlooked, my benefits and rewards will come from You!

Promise-Power Point: God has rewards and bonuses for me that I can only receive when I use my time, talents, and treasure to bless someone else.

Our Savior in the Storm

"No, I will not abandon you or leave you as orphans in the storm — I will come to you." John 14:18 TLB

When I first found out recently that I needed surgery, I was devastated. For many months, I had prayed and trusted God to heal me without surgery, and I believed with all my heart that He would spare me from it. As I waited for my surgery date, I earnestly sought the Lord in prayer and Scripture reading, as was my habit for many years. God helped me to work through my disappointment and disillusionment, and to prepare me for trusting Him for a speedy recovery after my operation. But there were still those moments when I wrestled with doubt and despair.

One morning, the Lord led me to a passage in Mark 4, where Jesus and His disciples were in a boat that was filling up with water, because of a fierce storm causing high winds and waves. Jesus Himself was sound asleep on a cushion, when the disciples woke Him up and shouted, "Don't You care that we're going to drown?" (Mark 4:38 NLT) I had a good idea of how the disciples must have felt that day. My own heart's cry had been, "Lord, don't You care that I am suffering? Don't You care that I need surgery?" The next thing this passage of Scripture tells us is that Jesus got up and rebuked the winds and waves, saying, "Peace, be still". (Mark 4:39

NKJV)   That's when the Holy Spirit brought to my remembrance the Lord's promise in John 14:18 (TLB), where He tells His beloved followers, "No, I will not abandon you or leave you as orphans in the storm — I will come to you." This was the Savior's way of saying, "Be at peace and just trust Me. I will be with you all the way. I will never leave you nor forsake you." After Jesus rebuked the winds and the waves, He rebuked His disciples, asking, "Why are you so afraid? Do you still have no faith?" (Mark 4:40 NIV) I can imagine the hurt in the Savior's heart and voice as He spoke the words to His loved ones.

Just as the Lord calmed the storm for His disciples that day, He wants to calm the storms that come into my life and yours. But we have to trust Him. That means that if we have prayed for protection, healing, and deliverance, but our prayers have not been answered the way we had hoped, then we must believe that God has a purpose for our difficulty, and that it's a good purpose. No matter what you are going through today, I urge you not to forfeit the blessings that the Lord has for you by giving in to discouragement and despair. Trust Him. Lean heavily on Him. And watch Him reveal the treasure in your trial.

Lord, I thank You that when I go through troubles and trials, I am not alone. Grant me Your discernible presence during those times when I am fearful and fretful. Quiet and calm my heart and mind, and give me the faith to stand strong. Today, I choose to put my trust in You, and to believe that You are a good God, and You will turn my disappointments into blessings!

Promise-Power Point: As I refuse to give in to doubt and despair in troubled times, the Lord will make His presence known, and He will calm both me and my storms.

The Fear of Man

"The fear of human opinion disables; trusting God protects you from that." Proverbs 29:25 MSG

In the tenth chapter of the Gospel of Matthew, we find Jesus instructing His disciples about their relationship with God and others – especially with regard to their fear of man versus their fear of God. If we take the Master's teachings to heart, we just may find ourselves enjoying more peace, joy, and freedom than ever before. As the Lord sends His disciples out into the world, He tells them: "Behold, I send you out as sheep in the midst of wolves; so be shrewd as serpents and innocent as doves." (Matthew 10:16 NASB) This has been some of the most valuable advice I have ever gotten from the Scriptures. On the one hand, it has helped me to avoid having a suspicious mind toward others, and on the other hand, it has reminded me that God doesn't want me to be a doormat, or to let people take advantage of me. Jesus issues us a stern warning in the next verse when He says, "Be on your guard against men." (10:17 NIV)

Unfortunately, some of the people we are going to be in conflict with, because of our devotion to Christ, will be members of our own family. As Jesus says: "Do not suppose that I have come to bring peace to the earth. I did not come to bring peace, but a sword. For I have come to turn 'a man against his father, a daughter against her mother, a daughter-in-law against her mother-in-law – a man's enemies will be the members of his own household.'" (Matthew 10:34-36 NIV) The Lord is not condemning earthly ties, but He makes it clear that they should not be allowed to divert or distract us from aggressively following Him wherever He leads. He warns us that our loyalty to Him will cause some of our own loved ones to turn their backs on us. And He goes on to say: "Anyone who loves his father or mother more than Me is not worthy of Me; anyone who loves his son or daughter more than Me is not worthy of Me; and anyone who does not take his cross and follow Me is not worthy of Me." (Matthew 10:37-38 NIV) Following Christ means putting Him above all of our relatives, friends, and loved ones, and making the sacrifices He calls us to in order to obey His will.

Included in this chapter are some encouraging words from the Savior. He reminds us that He was the first to suffer rejection and persecution, and we shouldn't be surprised when His followers suffer the same fate. (Matthew 10:24-25) And He teaches us the difference between worldly fear and godly fear. "Don't be afraid of those who want to kill your body; they cannot touch your soul. Fear only God, who can destroy both soul and body in hell." (Matthew 10:28 NLT) Here, Jesus condemns the fear of man, and upholds the fear of God. It is God alone who will determine our final destiny, and it is He who deserves our reverential fear and awe.

Proverbs 29:25 (NLT) says: "Fearing people is a dangerous trap, but trusting the Lord means safety." How many rewards and blessings do we miss out on because we allow others to frighten or intimidate us? How many promotions and opportunities do we forfeit because we allow feelings of fear and panic to control us? God can't use us the way He wants to when we live timid, fearful lives. The fear of man paralyzes us and imprisons us; the fear of God liberates us and sets us free. One of the things I have learned to appreciate most about serving God wholeheartedly all these years is that I no longer have to worry about what others think. In every situation, all I have to do is seek His perspective and will in the matter – and follow His lead – and I can enjoy the peace and well-being Jesus died for me to have.

The Lord wants to use you in greater ways, and bless you beyond your wildest dreams. Are you prepared to shun the fear of man, and give Him the reverential fear and awe that He deserves?

Lord, forgive me for the times I worried more about what others thought than what You thought. Deliver me from a fear of people that paralyzes, and fill me with a godly fear that enables, empowers, and overcomes. Remind me often that in every battle, You will fight for me and uphold my cause if I will wait on You and follow Your lead. Thank You that as I put You and Your purposes first, I will have Your supernatural favor and victory!

Promise-Power Point: God offers me freedom from intimidation and manipulation, but in order to secure that freedom, I must do my part by using His wisdom in relating to others, and focusing on pleasing Him and putting Him first.

The God Who Hears and Answers

"You hear, O Lord, the desire of the afflicted; You encourage them, and You listen to their cry." Psalm 10:17 NIV

This three-fold promise is one that I have stood on hundreds of times in all my years of walking closely with the Lord.   It's especially dear to me when I'm going through dark and difficult times.

First, God promises that when we are afflicted, or suffering, in any way, He will hear the desires of our hearts.   But I have found that the Lord often wants us to voice those desires to Him, and to make them specific.   If we look at Jesus throughout the Gospels, many times, when people came to Him with a need, He asked them, "What do you want Me to do for you?" (Mark 10:51 NIV)   The interesting thing about these occasions is that when the needy people involved called upon Jesus, it was pretty obvious to everyone there what these hurting people wanted.   Yet, Jesus asked them to tell Him specifically what they desired.   Too often, believers have the attitude, "Well, God knows all things, so why should I have to tell Him what I want?" This is the wrong attitude for Christ-followers to have. The Lord wants us to come to Him in humble dependence, and to ask Him for the desires of our hearts.   When we do, we open the door for God to do in our lives and circumstances what only He can do.

Next, the Lord promises encouragement when we need it most. The Bible says that God gives encouragement. (Romans 15:5) And I often hear myself praying, "Lord, please send me some special encouragement now." Sometimes, He sends someone across my path to speak words of comfort and strength to me. Other times, He supplies the encouragement I need directly through His own Spirit in me. Be sensitive to those times when you could use some extra support, and ask the Lord to send you a much-needed lift.

Finally, this promise says that God listens to our cries. Sometimes, we can be hurting so badly that all we can say is, "Lord, help me!" Sometimes, that will be enough. While it can really benefit us to voice our specific needs and desires in prayer, the fact is that in our humanity, there will be times when we are just not able. The Bible says, "He does not ignore the cry of the afflicted". (Psalm 9:12 NIV) Don't believe the devil's lies that God won't hear your cries when you are in trouble. Even if you caused your own miseries, when you cry out to Him for help – especially when you call on the name of Jesus – you can bet that the Lord will act on your behalf somehow. What is it that you would most like to say to the God who hears and answers today?

Lord, teach me how to express my desires to You when I am hurting in any way. Remind me to ask You to send me encouragement and support whenever I need it. Don't let me be deceived into thinking that You won't hear me when I cry out to You. Thank You for being a God who sees, hears, and cares!

Promise-Power Point: In times of hardship and heartache, if I will cry out to God, ask Him for the desires of my heart, and pray for encouragement, He will lift me up and give me all the relief and resources I need.

You Don't Need Any Helpers

"So we say with confidence, 'The Lord is my helper; I will not be afraid.'" Hebrews 13:6 NIV

Recently, I had one of those days when my relationship with my husband, Joe, was sorely tested. With houseguests soon to arrive at our house, I was really counting on him to help me with some major chores. Unfortunately, he chose to begin working on another project that had absolutely no bearing on our imminent houseguests and their comfort. I expressed my desire to my husband to have his help with the cleaning, but my requests fell on deaf ears.

As I turned to the Lord in silent prayer, I confessed that I was struggling with anger and frustration. That's when I heard Him speak to my spirit, "You don't need any helpers. All you need is Me." Now, I know that God is not against us asking for help when we need it. But what He was telling me here was that when I ask for help, and my request is refused or ignored, I don't have to get angry or vengeful. Instead, I can bring the situation before God, and He will supply all the help I need – whether He uses someone else, or gives me all the skills, energy, and strength I need to accomplish the task myself.

As I set about my work for the day on my own, the Lord reminded me of His Word in Hebrews 13:6 (NIV): "So we say with confidence, 'The Lord is my helper; I will not be afraid.'" I'll be honest and tell you that I still was not happy about having to do all that work alone. But because I was determined to resist getting mad or vindictive toward my husband, God gave me all the help I needed to complete the task, and to do it beautifully. You, too, have a divine Helper who is there for you when you call on Him. If you are in a place of need right now, let Him hear from you today!

Lord, forgive me for the times that others refused to help me when I was in need, and I failed to respond with a Christlike attitude. Guard me from the bitterness and unforgiveness that can hinder my prayers, and make it difficult for me to hear from You clearly. Give me a heart like Yours, and help me to quickly and thoroughly forgive those who hurt or offend me. Thank You that as I obey You in this area, You will give me all the strength and wisdom I need to accomplish all that You have called me to!

Promise-Power Point: When others fail to help me when I am in need, if I remain kind and confident, and lean on the Lord, He will equip me to do whatever I need to do with supernatural joy, skill, and efficiency!

Good News vs. Bad News

"A cheerful look brings joy to the heart; good news makes for good health." *Proverbs 15:30 NLT*

Many years ago, when I was receiving counseling for anxiety and depression, my therapist warned me not to watch or listen to broadcasts of the news. To this very day, I remember her telling me, "It's not good for you." We live in an age when we are bombarded with news – almost all of it negative – and it's harming our mental, emotional, physical, and spiritual health. When people find out that I don't make a habit of listening to the news, they politely accuse me of "sticking my head in the sand". In other words, they view me as uninformed and out of touch. I might have taken offense by comments like these years ago, but now I know better.

Perhaps you know some folks who like to listen to negative, and even provocative, news, and who derive a perverse pleasure from telling it to others. These people have no problem listening to gruesome details about heinous crimes committed against innocent people, including children. They aren't satisfied taking this kind of poison themselves, but they want to share it with others. But this practice is an insult and offense to God, because His Word says, "It is shameful even to talk about the things that ungodly people do in secret." (Ephesians 5:12 NLT)

Solomon wrote, "Good news makes for good health." (Proverbs 15:30 NLT) And I submit to you that bad news makes for bad health. I have experienced these principles and truths firsthand, and so today I take every opportunity I can to warn others. What we listen to will affect our thinking. And our thinking will determine our destiny. God's Word says: "Fix your thoughts on what is true, and honorable, and right, and pure, and lovely, and admirable. Think about things that are excellent and worthy of praise." (Philippians 4:8 NLT) It's no coincidence that this verse comes from a passage that the Apostle Paul wrote instructing us how to have peace of mind and heart.

I once heard a godly man talking about this very subject, and he exclaimed, "My ears are not garbage cans!" If you want to experience more peace and well-being, then take this message to heart today. It could save you a lot of trouble and turmoil.

Lord, I no longer want to be careless about what and who I listen to. Open my eyes so that I may see and understand just how destructive negative reports can be to my health and well-being. Remind me often that You have commanded me to "be wise about what is good, and innocent about what is evil." (Romans 16:19 NIV) Thank You that as I obey You in this area, I will experience more peace, joy, and vibrant health than ever before!

Promise-Power Point: When I make it a point to fill my life with good news – especially the Good News in God's Word – I will be able to claim the "good health" that the Lord promises.

About the Author

Since 1998, **J. M. Farro** has served as the Devotional Writer and Prayer Counselor for Jesusfreakhideout.com – one of the first and largest Christian music web sites in the world. Her mission is to help others to discover the life-changing power of having a deeply personal relationship with Christ.

Through devotionals, podcasts, blogs, and books – including the best-selling *Life on Purpose* devotional book series – she encourages others to fulfill their God-given purpose and potential. She and her husband, Joe, have two sons, and live in Nazareth, Pennsylvania.

J. M. Farro
P.O. Box 434
Nazareth, PA 18064

jmf@jmfarro.com
farro@jesusfreakhideout.com

www.jmfarro.com
www.jesusfreakhideout.com
www.littlejesusfreaks.com

NOTES

NOTES

31689165R00119

Made in the USA
Charleston, SC
25 July 2014